NORWEGIAN
Verbs & Essentials of Grammar

A PRACTICAL GUIDE TO THE MASTERY
OF NORWEGIAN

NORWEGIAN
Verbs & Essentials of Grammar

Louis Janus

New York   Chicago   San Francisco   Lisbon   London   Madrid   Mexico City
Milan   New Delhi   San Juan   Seoul   Singapore   Sydney   Toronto

Library of Congress Cataloging-in-Publication Data

Janus, Louis.
    Norwegian verbs & essentials of grammar : a practical guide to the mastery of
Norwegian / Louis Janus.
       p.   cm.
    Includes index.
    ISBN 0-8442-8596-X
       1. Norwegian language—Verb.   2. Norwegian language—Grammar.
I. Title.   II. Title: Norwegian verbs & essentials of grammar.
PD2661.J36   1998
439'.682421—dc21   98-43328
                                            CIP

11 12 13 14 15 16 17 18 19 20 21 22 23 24 WFR / WFR 0

ISBN 978-0-8442-8596-2
MHID   0-8442-8596-X

Cover design by Nick Panos
Interior design and composition by VARDA Graphics

McGraw-Hill books are available at special quantity discounts to use as premiums
and sales promotions or for use in corporate training programs. To contact a
representative, please visit the Contact Us pages at www.mhprofessional.com.

This book is printed on acid-free paper.

Contents

Preface

Norwegian Verbs & Essentials of Grammar presents the major grammatical concepts of the Norwegian language. As evidenced by the first section of this book, major emphasis is given to the mastery of verbs, their conjugations, and uses. Grammar and sentence structure are presented in easily understood contexts. New material is introduced in such a way that it is based upon previously learned material, so that the student can progress with ease through the various sections. Each individual grammatical point is dealt with step-by-step, enabling the student to fully grasp a concept before moving on.

The major advantage of *Norwegian Verbs & Essentials of Grammar* is that complete grammatical explanations are contained in one section and not scattered throughout the text. Therefore, teacher and student can easily find specific information.

Following each explanation of verb forms or grammar are numerous examples. These clearly illustrate the point in question and can be used as a basis for further work by the student. The list of verbs provides material for use in creative exercises, oral presentations, and compositions.

As a reference text, *Norwegian Verbs & Essentials of Grammar* can be used by the individual student for study or review, or by the teacher and class as a supplement to any of the basic textbooks. Because of the logical order in which concepts are presented, this book can be used at both the college and the adult education levels.

1 Introduction to the Norwegian Language

A Brief History of Norwegian

Norwegian is a North Germanic language, related closely enough to Swedish and Danish as to be mutually intelligible with the two. Icelandic, the other North Germanic language, is also related, but not mutually intelligible. Since English and German are West Germanic languages, they share many features with Norwegian, including a cognate basic vocabulary and similar sentence structure. In addition to having similar family histories, Norwegian shares a large part of its vocabulary with German and English through later borrowings. Knowing either English or German is a definite advantage in learning Norwegian.

During the four hundred years when Norway was essentially ruled from Denmark, the standard written form of Norwegian died out. While the people of Norway continued to speak their own dialects, Danish was the official language of church, state, and culture. When Norway gained independence from Denmark in 1814, many felt that the official language should be modified to more closely reflect dialectal forms that had continued to evolve. In the mid 1800s, two approaches to modifying written Norwegian were followed, leading the way to the two standard written forms used today. *Bokmål*, the written form in this book, and the language spoken by most Norwegians in the East and North, is sometimes called Dano-Norwegian, and it was previously referred to as *Rigsmaal* or *Riksmål*, "the language of the realm." This standard written form evolved directly from Danish, with variant spellings that better represented Norwegian pronunciation and grammatical forms (forms used throughout Norway, but not in Denmark). *Nynorsk* (previously called *Landsmaal* or *Landsmål*) was a revolutionary replacement for the written Danish based on the pioneering linguistic work of Ivar Aasen. Aasen traveled throughout western Norway and reconstructed what the language might have looked like had it not been influenced for such a long time by Danish. A parliamentary resolution in 1885 established *Bokmål* and *Nynorsk* as equal written standards, and all official publications must still be made available in both. These two are only written forms; the spoken language continues to be based on regional dialects, which may resemble either *Bokmål* or *Nynorsk* more closely for each native speaker. Currently, Norwegian is spoken as a first language by almost 4½ million inhabitants of the country.

This book describes the verbs and grammar of *Bokmål*, the form that is more commonly learned by non-Norwegians. In Norway, local school districts determine which standard written form will be taught first. All students must pass tests in both *Bokmål* and *Nynorsk*. Slightly under 83 percent of all Norwegian elementary school pupils are taught *Bokmål* before *Nynorsk*. In 1994, several *fylker* (counties) in Norway had no schools with *Nynorsk* as their primary language (Østfold, Akershus, Oslo, Vestfold, Nordland, Troms, Finnmark, and Svalbard). Sogn og Fjordane was the *fylke* with the highest percentage of *Nynorsk* pupils: 96 percent.

Bokmål and Nynorsk Compared

This short text from a Norwegian folktale shows some differences between *Bokmål* and *Nynorsk*. The table reviews these and other differences.

Bokmål:

Det var en gang en gris som bodde tett ved en kongsgård. Så var det en dag at alle de andre var i kirke. Da syntes grisen det ble stusslig, og så rusla han oppover til kongsgården.

Nynorsk:

Det var ein gong ein gris som budde tett attmed ein kongsgard. Så var det ein dag alle dei andre var i kyrkja, og då tykte grisen det vart stussleg, og så rusla han i veg opp til kongsgarden.

English:

Once upon a time there was a pig who lived near the king's estate. It so happened that one day everyone was in church. The pig thought it was getting lonesome, and so he shuffled up toward the royal estate.

(Text from Anton Fjeldstad, *Lærebok i norsk for svensker,* Studentlitteratur, Lund 1972; used with permission of publisher.)

Nature of Difference	Bokmål	Nynorsk	English
Some specific lexical differences	Norge, jeg, hun, ikke, forskjell	Noreg, eg, ho, ikkje, skilnad	Norway, I, she, not, difference
Nynorsk requires more nouns to use the feminine gender (ei) forms. Bokmål usually allows a choice.	boken or boka en bok or ei bok	boka ei bok	the book a book
Bokmål allows most neuter definite plurals to end in -ene or -a. Nynorsk requires -a.	husene or husa eplene or epla	husa epla	the houses the apples
Nynorsk uses more diphthongs. Bokmål often allows a choice.	et, vet or veit øst or aust	eit, veit aust	a, knows east
Nynorsk uses consonant cluster kv where Bokmål uses hv.	hva, hvit	kva, kvit	what, white
Nynorsk has a vowel alternation for strong verbs in the present tense and no -r ending.	sover kommer	søv kjem	sleeps comes
Nynorsk uses unstressed a in many words where Bokmål uses e.	stoler kaster gammel	stolar kastar gammal	chairs throws old
Bokmål uses the pronoun den to refer to en or ei gender inanimate objects, Nynorsk uses han or ho.	Har du en sykkel? Nei, jeg har solgt den.	Har du en sykkel? Nei, eg har selt han.	Do you have a bicycle? No, I've sold it.

Variation Within Bokmål

Both *Nynorsk* and *Bokmål* allow some options in choosing word forms. The 38 members of the Norwegian Language Council (*Språkråd*) determine acceptable forms, having set up a two-tiered system in 1938. Many words on the official lists have both a principal form and optional forms. Words can have several equal-status principal forms (for example, **boken/boka** "the book," **synes/syns** "seems, thinks"). Optional forms are allowed in students' writings, while principal forms are required in textbooks and official government documents. For example, the past tense form of **å gi** "to give" has the principal **ga** with optional **gav** "gave."

2 Alphabet

Norwegian uses the same 26 letters as English plus three additional vowels, alphabetized after *z:* **æ, ø, å**. These vowels are occasionally (in library catalogs and electronic documents) represented by **ae, oe,** and **aa.** The letters **c, q, x,** and **z** are rarely used in words native to Norwegian.

In this book, the pronunciation of words and letters is represented between slashes using the International Phonetic Alphabet (IPA). Readers will note the differences between English and Norwegian pronunciation. For example, the printed *g* in Norwegian is sometimes pronounced as English /g/, but at other times as /j/.

The names of the letters as represented using the International Phonetic Alphabet are shown between forward slashes. Long vowels are represented with a colon (for example, /i:/).

a	/ɑ:/	**k**	/kɔ:/
b	/be:/	**l**	/el/
c	/se:/	**m**	/em/
d	/de:/	**n**	/en/
e	/e:/	**o**	/ɯ:/
f	/ef/	**p**	/pe:/
g	/ge:/	**q**	/kʉ:/
h	/hɔ:/	**r**	/ær/
i	/i:/	**s**	/es/
j	/je:/ or /jɔdd/	**t**	/te:/

u	/ʉː/		z	/sett/
v	/veː/		æ	/æː/
w	/dɔbbelt veː/		ø	/øː/
x	/eks/		å	/ɔː/
y	/yː/			

Norwegian uses a few accented vowels, showing stress on the syllable with the accent mark. This is different from French where accents change vowel sounds. The most common (yet still quite rare) accent is é, as in kafé "café" or orkidé "orchid." A handful of words use ò, seen in the strongly stressed adverb òg "also," which only occurs at the end of sentences. The French preposition à is used in expressions with numbers like 3 kg à kr 5 "3 kilograms at 5 kroner per kilo." The words fôr "feed" and fór "traveled" (past tense of å fare) are differentiated from the common adverb and preposition for "too, for."

3 Pronunciation

Vowels

There are nine simple vowels, or monophthongs in Norwegian, each of which may be pronounced with either long or short duration: /ɑ, e, i, ɯ, ʉ, y, æ, ø, ɔ/. When monophthongs are pronounced as long vowels, their pronunciation is of a longer duration and with tenser tongue and lips. The difference in vowel length is often the only way to distinguish otherwise similar words.

In addition to the nine monophthongs, Norwegian has five diphthongs: /æⁱ, øʸ, æᵘ, ɔʸ, and ʉʸ/. A diphthong is considered a single vowel sound, but it is composed of two vowel elements. The second vowel sometimes feels like an "offglide" from the first. Three of the Norwegian diphthongs are fairly common, while the other two should be mentioned for the sake of completeness, but need not cause undue concern for students. The diphthongs will be discussed after the nine monophthongs below.

It is impossible to give good directions in print alone on how to pronounce a foreign language. The best any written text can do is to make suggestions about similar sounds in English. Below are such suggestions, although the student is advised to make every attempt possible at finding and imitating either recorded speech or a native speaker of Norwegian. The table below gives the IPA symbols for all long vowels and diphthongs in Norwegian, a description of tongue and lip positions, and a near-equivalent sound in English. The corresponding short vowels are pronounced with less lip and tongue energy, and written without the colon (:).

Monophthong	Tongue and Lip Positions	English Near Equivalents	Norwegian Examples
/ɑ:/	low, back, unrounded	father	**far** father **dager** days

/e:/	mid, front, unrounded; tendency to have /ə/ offglide	halfway between *sad* and *said*	**h<u>e</u>ter** be named **tre** three, tree
/i:/	high, front, unrounded	bee	**min** my **si** say
/ɯ:/	high, back, over-rounded	more rounded than *moo*	**noe** any **to** two
/ʉ:/	central, high, over-rounded	you	**du** you **Gud** God
/y:/	high, front, over-rounded	no English equivalent; start with /i:/ and purse lips	**by** city **sky** cloud
/æ:/	mid, front, unrounded	bag	**er** am, is, are **ære** honor
/ø:/	mid, back, rounded	bird (without the *r* sound)	**øve** practice **høre** hear
/ɔ:/ (written /å:/ in this book)	low, central, rounded	eastern U.S. and British *awe*	**år** year **håpe** hope

Diphthong	**Monophthong Progression**	**English Near Equivalents**	**Norwegian Examples**
/æⁱ/	start with /æ/ and rise to /i/	halfway between English *hey* and *hi*	**jeg** I **bein** bone, leg
/øʸ/	start with /ø/ and rise to /y/	close to English *boy*	**høyre** right **øye** eye
/æᵘ/	start with /æ/ then rise and round to /ʉ/	similar to English *ow*, in *cow* or *how*	**tau** rope **Europa** Europe

| /ɔʸ/ | start with /å/ and rise to /y/ | very similar to *oy* in English *boy* | **konvoi** convoy **boikott** boycott |
| /aⁱ/ | start with /a/ and glide to /i/ | similar to English *i* in *high* | **hai** shark |

Consonants

The following Norwegian consonants are pronounced very much like their English equivalents: /b, d, f, h, l, m, n, p, s, t, v/. The main differences between the two are in the remaining consonants, as discussed below. In a manner similar to vowels, consonants in Norwegian can also be long or short, with long consonants generally following short vowels in stressed syllables.

Word Stress and Vowel Length

Most native Norwegian words are stressed on their first syllables. Borrowed terms often imitate the lending language's syllable stress (for example, **restaurant** "restaurant" is stressed on the final syllable, as it is in French and other European languages). Prefixes like **be-** (e.g., **betale** "pay") and **for-** (**forandre** "change") are not stressed.

Stressed syllables in Norwegian generally can have a long vowel followed by a short consonant (e.g., **tok** /tuː:k/ "took"), a long vowel followed by no consonant (**ta** /tɑ:/ "take"), or a short vowel followed by a long consonant or consonant group (**takk** /tɑk/ "thanks").

In unstressed syllables, vowels maintain their quality, but are always short. Here English differs in that speakers tend to reduce the quality of unstressed vowels to a *schwa* /ə/ as in the casual pronunciation of words like *monotony, triangular,* and *permanent.* Carryover of this tendency may cause problems for English speakers who often reduce the final unstressed syllable in Norwegian words, neglecting the difference between words like **jente** /jentə/ "girl" and **jenta** /jenta/ "the girl."

In addition to its relation to word stress, vowel length is largely predictable from the spelling of a word. Short vowels are generally followed by two or more consonants, whereas long vowels are followed by single consonants. For example, **tak** /tɑ:k/ "roof" has a long /ɑ:/ but **takk** /tɑk/ "thanks" has a short /ɑ/.

Vowel length and quality are thus very important features of spoken Norwegian. The student is urged to listen to native speakers and imitate—perhaps even exaggerate—the distinctions.

Tones and Intonation

Many non-Norwegians remark on the singsong quality of spoken Norwegian. Two features of the language aid in creating this impression: wordtone and sentence intonation.

All stressed words in spoken East Norwegian have either a rising tone (sometimes called single tone) or a falling tone followed by a rising tone (double tone). In West Norway, the double tone rises, then falls. The actual manifestation of these tones varies considerably throughout the dialect areas, but all spoken Norwegian contrasts single and double tones in stressed words. The origins of this feature of the language are deeply rooted in the history of the Germanic languages, and can account for different meanings in otherwise similar words: **været** "the weather" is pronounced with single tone, with the syllable **vær-** lower in pitch than the syllable /e/ (the **t** of the definite ending is silent). Contrast that word with **være** "be," which has a double tone pronunciation, but is otherwise identical.

The other prosodic feature of spoken Norwegian that catches the ear of non-Norwegians is the sentence melody or intonation. In East Norwegian, the last word or word group in a declarative sentence ends higher than the rest of the sentence. The overall effect sounds to many English speakers like a question, and they are often left wondering why Norwegians make so many inquiries. When Norwegians do want to ask questions, the speaker's intonation has an even sharper rise on the last word than it would in a statement.

Distinctive Norwegian Sounds

Vowels

Several Norwegian vowel sounds are made with rounded lips, and as such are not customarily produced by English speakers. /y/ and /y:/ are like /i/ and /i:/ except that the lips are drawn forward and rounded. /ø/ and /ø:/ are rounded versions of /e/ and /e:/. /ɑ̊/ and /ɑ̊:/ are similar to /ɑ/ and /ɑ:/, but with rounded lips.

Consonants

Several consonant clusters (groups of two or more consonants) are never seen in English but are common in Norwegian. As examples, the **bj** as in **bjørn** "bear" and **fj** as in **fjord** start with the /b/ or /f/ and make a quick "offglide" to a short /i/ or /y/ sound. The English words *beauty* and *future* have initial sounds very similar to these Norwegian clusters.

Both letters **k** and **g** have two distinct pronunciations. Before back vowels **a, å, o,** and **u,** these consonants are pronounced with their "hard" sounds in a manner similar to English; for example, **kål** /kå:l/ "cabbage." Before the front vowels **i, y,** and **ø,** the **k** has a softer, fricative sound, which corresponds to the spelling **kj** /ç/; for example, **kirke** /çirkə/ "church," **kino** /çi:nɯ/ "movie," **kylling** /çylliŋ/ "chicken." Before the front vowels **i, y,** and **ø,** the written consonant **g** is pronounced as /j/: **gi** /ji:/ "give," **begynne** /bejynnə/ "begin."

Several written clusters share the sound pronounced /ʃ/ (similar to the initial sound in English *she*). The most common groups are: **sj, ski, skj,** and **rs** as in the following words: **sju** /ʃʉ:/ "seven," **ski** /ʃi:/ "ski," **skje** /ʃe:/ "spoon," and **norsk** /nåʃk/ "Norwegian."

East and North Norwegian /r/ is a tap, flap, or trill using the tip of the tongue against the alveolar ridge, directly behind the front teeth. The American English /r/ sounds are very different, pronounced as retroflex sounds, with the root of the tongue pulled back towards the soft palate. Along the south and west coast of Norway, the /r/ sound is uvular, very similar to a French /r/, and still unlike the American English retroflex /r/.

Relating Spelling to Pronunciation

In general, Norwegian is pronounced much more closely to the way it is spelled than English is. By noticing a few patterns, the new speaker can become quite proficient at guessing how to say a word after reading it.

Here follow some hints about the relationship of spelling to the pronunciation of vowels:

1. Often the letter **o** when followed by two or more consonants is pronounced as the vowel sound /å/. **Godt** "good, well" is pronounced as /gått/. **Norsk** "Norwegian" uses the short /å/ vowel.
2. **e** before **r** is often pronounced /æ/: **er** /æ:r/, **der** /dæ:r/ "there."
3. The diphthong /æi/ can be written with the following combinations:
   -eg as in **jeg** /jæi/ "I"
   -egn as in **regn** /ræin/ "rain"
   -ei as in **bein** /bæin/ "leg, bone"

"Silent" Letters

Some common spellings in Norwegian contain elements that *are not* pronounced: "silent" letters.

1. **-ig** is pronounced /i/. The printed **g** is not pronounced. Many adjectives and adverbs end in **-ig** or **-lig,** e.g., **hyggelig** /hyggeli/ "pleasant."

2. Interrogatives corresponding to English *wh-* words are spelled with **hv-** and pronounced /v/, e.g., **hva** /vɑ:/ "what," **hvor** /vor/ "where." Other words that start with **hv-** are pronounced with /v/: **hvite** "white" and **hvete** "wheat."

3. **Hj-** is always pronounced /j/, e.g., **hjemme** /jemmə/ "at home," **hjelpe** /jelpə/ "help," and **hjørnet** /jørnə/ "the corner."

4. **Gj-** is always pronounced as /j/: **gjøre** /jørə/ "do," **gjennom** /jennåm/ "through."

5. **-t** is not pronounced in the pronoun or demonstrative **det**, which should always be pronounced /de:/.

6. **-t** as part of the definite ending of **et** nouns is not pronounced in normal speech, although some very careful speakers may use this learned pronunciation. For most speakers, **huset** "the house" is pronounced /husə/. However, the final written **-t** is pronounced when it comes as the past tense or past participle ending on verbs: **snakket** /snakket/ "spoke, spoken."

7. **-d** is often not pronounced at the end of several "small words" like **med** /me:/ "with," **ved** /ve:/ "at."

8. The conjunction **og** "and" is almost always pronounced /å/ without a /g/ sound in casual and informal Norwegian. However, careful Norwegian speakers frequently use a pronunciation like /å:g/. In the stressed adverb **òg** "also" the *g* is pronounced.

9. There is no voiced /z/ sound in Norwegian. In borrowed terms like **Zulu** "Zulu," Norwegian uses a voiceless /s/, i.e., /sʉ:lʉ/.

4 Spelling Conventions in Norwegian

English has some rules that monitor changes in spelling for various forms of a word. For example, we double the final *p* before adding endings to words like *stop: stopped, stopping.* We also change the final **y** to **i** before adding endings: *fly–flies, modify–modification.* Norwegian has similar conventions that regulate the written language.

1 No Final -mm

Norwegian words never end in **-mm,** but **-mm-** frequently occurs in the middle of words. Often a word ends in single **-m** in one form, but uses **-mm-** when it is not the last letter in a related word. Note that spelling conventions apply generally to words, and are not restricted to one part of speech.

et rom a room	**rommet** the room
hjem to home	**hjemme** at home
morsom fun (singular)	**morsomme** fun (plural)
kom come, came (imperative, past tense)	**komme** come (infinitive)

Some words end in a single consonant because the vowel that precedes it is long. To preserve vowel length, the word-final consonant is not doubled with the addition of an ending. For example, the noun **et problem** "a problem" retains only one **-m** when an ending is added: **problemet** "the problem," to preserve its pronunciation, /proble:m/.

2   Avoid Three Consecutive Consonants

The Norwegian tendency is to avoid three consonants in a row. If a consonant can be dropped without the word becoming confused with others, this is usually done. The adjective **grønn** "green," for example, adds the consonant ending **-t** for a neuter singular noun. The form then is **grønt,** rather than ***grønnt.** Other examples include adding the past tense ending to a verb: **å kjenne** "to know," **kjente** "knew;" **å glemme** "to forget," **glemte** "forgot;" **å spille** "to play," **spilte** "played."

3   Drop Unstressed -e

In unstressed syllables, the vowel **-e** is often dropped when an ending is added, especially in combinations like **-el, -en,** and **-er.** For example, in nouns, **en onkel** "uncle" (singular) corresponds to **onkler** "uncles" (plural); **ei finger** "a finger," **fingrer** "fingers;" **et teater** "a theater," **teatret** "the theater." This spelling convention is applied also to adjectives; for example, **gammel** "old" (singular), **gamle** "old" (plural and definite).

4   Accented -é

A very small number of Norwegian words use the acute accent **-é,** for example in **kafé** "café" and **orkidé** "orchid." In a word like **idé** "idea," the accent is not used when endings are added: **en idé, ideen** "the idea," **ideer** "ideas," and **ideene** "the ideas."

---

*The asterisk denotes that the form is wrong and should not be used.

Part One

Norwegian
Verbs

5 Overview of Verb Forms

The Norwegian verbal system is generally simpler than that of many other European languages. Within each tense, all subjects have the same form. Compare English present tense "am/is/are" to Norwegian, where the form is **er** throughout:

I am	**Jeg er**
You (informal—singular) are	**Du er**
You (formal—singular and plural) are	**De er**
He, she, it is	**Han, hun, den / det er**
We are	**Vi er**
You (informal—plural) are	**Dere er**
They are	**De er**

Infinitive

The infinitive is a form of the verb that does not appear in a specific tense or time. These verb forms often appear with the infinitive marker: "to" in English and **å** in Norwegian. All Norwegian infinitives end in vowels, except a few infinitives of **-s** verbs (see chapter 14). Examples of infinitives (shown here with the infinitive marker) are: **å tenke** "to think," **å bære** "to carry, bear," **å treffe** "to meet," **å gjøre** "to do," **å si** "to say," **å se** "to see," **å bo** "to dwell." The infinitive is the name of the action, and as such may be used as a noun, as the subject of a sentence:

Å prate med venner er hyggelig.   To chat with friends is pleasant.

Infinitives can also function as objects, as seen in constructions such as:

Jeg liker å spille ishockey.   I like to play hockey.

Marit er glad i å snakke norsk.   Marit is fond of speaking
                                        Norwegian.

The infinitive (without the marker **å**) is used with modal helping verbs such as **må, måtte, kan, kunne** (see discussion of modals in chapter 7):

Dere må lese nå.   You must read now.

Kunne du sende meg saltet?   Could you pass me the salt?

Stem

For many of the forms of verbs discussed in these chapters, it is important to know what a verb's stem is. The stem is the infinitive minus the unstressed **-e** at the end (if there is one). For verbs that end in stressed vowels, the stem is the same as the infinitive:

Infinitive	Stem
kjøpe	kjøp
oversette	oversett
selge	selg
gå	gå
bli	bli

Imperative

The imperative form resembles the stem. It is used to command someone (an understood "you" subject) to do something.

Gå!   Go!

Snakk norsk!   Speak Norwegian!

Si det på engelsk.   Say it in English.

Sample Verb in All Tenses

Below is a chart of the verb **å spise** "to eat" in all forms. Note that these forms do not take different endings when used with different subjects. Norwegian verbs are uniform within a tense.

Infinitive	(å) spise	(to) eat
Stem	spis-	eat
Imperative	Spis!	Eat!
Present	spiser	eat/eats/eating
Past tense	spiste	ate
Present participle (used as adjective)	spisende	eating
Past participle	spist	eaten
Present perfect	har spist	has/have eaten
Past perfect	hadde spist	had eaten
-s passive	spises	is/are eaten
Bli + passive (present tense)	blir spist	is/are eaten
Future	skal/vil spise	shall/will eat
Conditional	skulle/ville spise	should/would eat

Verb Classes

Present tense forms in Norwegian show very little irregularity. The present tense is formed by adding **-r** to the infinitive (**å se** "to see," **han ser** "he sees"). There are only a handful of exceptions. (See the short list of irregular forms in chapter 6.) However, Norwegian past tense and participle forms can be divided into regular and irregular classes. When students understand the separation between regular and irregular past tense forms, and then the division of regular verbs into four classes, they find it much more efficient to learn the forms for each Norwegian verb.

Regular past tense forms use endings that consist of some combination of **-t** or **-d.** This is similar to English regular past tenses, which end in **-ed** (for example, *played* and *printed*). The four classes of past tense endings for regular verbs end in **-et, -te, -de,** and **-dde.** (See chapter 8 for a complete explanation of past tense forms.)

Corresponding endings for past participles for the four classes end in **-et, -t, -d,** and **-dd.** (Chapter 9 gives complete details on forming past participles.)

Verbs with past tenses and past participles that are not "regular" as described above are called "irregular." The forms for past tense and past participle for these verbs do not fall into neat classes, as do the forms for regular verbs. The forms for the past tense often have different vowels than the corresponding present tense and infinitive forms. Past tense forms for irregular verbs do not add **-t** or **-d** endings. English examples (that illustrate vowel changes) are "to write—she wrote; to eat—we ate." Norwegian examples include **å skrive** ("to write")—**hun skrev** ("she wrote") and **å drikke** ("to drink")—**vi drakk** ("we drank").

The fact that a verb is irregular in the past tense does not imply that it will be irregular in the present. For example **du drakk** ("you drank") shows an irregular verb form in the past tense, but the present tense form **du drikker** ("you are drinking") is regular.

6 Present Tense

Verb endings for all tenses are much simpler in Norwegian than in French, German, and even English because the endings in Norwegian are the same for all subjects. Norwegian verbs do not change according to the person or number of the subject: if you know the verb ending for one subject in Norwegian, you know the ending for all subjects. In addition, regular verbs far outnumber irregular verbs. However, as often happens in language, irregular verbs are among those most commonly used.

Forming the Present Tense

The present tense is used to describe events that are ongoing, repetitive, or habitual. Almost all verbs in Norwegian form the present tense (for all subjects) by adding an **-er** to the verb's stem (generally the infinitive minus an unstressed **-e** at the end—if there is one).

Regular Present Tense Forms

Infinitive	Subjects	Present tense
å bosette to settle	**jeg, du, han, hun, den, det, vi, dere, De, de, Georg, kvinnen...**	**bosetter** settles, settle
å ha to have	"	**har** has, have
å kjøpe to buy	"	**kjøper** buys, buy
å selge to sell	"	**selger** sells, sell

Irregular Present Tense Forms

Not counting the "-s verbs," only a handful of verbs have present tense forms that do not follow this pattern of adding -r, or -er to the stem:

Infinitive	Subjects	Present tense
å gjøre to do	jeg, du, han, hun, den, det, vi, dere, De, de, Georg, kvinnen...	gjør does, do
å spørre to ask	"	spør asks, ask
å være to be	"	er is, am, are
å vite to know a fact	"	vet knows, know

The following helping verbs (modal auxiliaries) also have irregular present tenses. Note that the equivalent English modals do not generally have infinitives (there is no form *to can,* or *to must*).

Infinitive	Subjects	Present tense
å kunne be able to	jeg, du, han, hun, den, det, vi, dere, De, de, Georg, kvinnen...	kan can
å ville to want to	"	vil wants to, want to
å måtte to need to	"	må must
å skulle should, shall	"	skal shall
å burde ought to	"	bør ought to

Examples of Present Tense Use

While English has three separate ways to describe an occurrence in the present, Norwegian uses one form:

She is eating.
She eats.   } **Hun spiser.**
She does eat.

Norwegian does not use the present progressive ("is eating") form. To stress the ongoing nature of an activity, two verbs are usually joined with **og:**

Mette sitter og leser.   Mette is reading [sitting and reading].

Extra emphasis as in the English "does eat" can be added with intonation or other markers.

Current activities

Jeg spiser middag nå.   I am eating dinner now.

Ann leser ei bok om irsk historie.   Ann is reading a book on Irish history.

Dette innlegget er jeg helt enig i.   I completely agree with this comment.

Kjell gjør mange interessante ting.   Kjell is doing many interesting things.

Vi er på besøk i Trondheim.   We are visiting Trondheim.

Bodil vet at Finn er hjemme.   Bodil knows that Finn is at home.

Usual or habitual states

Oslo er hovedstaden i Norge.   Oslo is the capital of Norway.

Vann koker ved 100° C.   Water boils at 100° Celsius.

Det er ikke gull alt som glimrer.   All that glitters is not gold.

Nordmenn snakker norsk.   Norwegians speak Norwegian.

Berit sover seint om søndagen.   Berit sleeps late on Sundays.

Petter og hans familie reiser til Italia hvert år.   Petter and his family travel to Italy every year.

Future activities

A present tense verb can be used to describe events that will take place in the future. An adverb or adverbial phrase indicates when in the future the event will take place.

Siri legger seg ved 11-tiden i kveld.	Siri will go to bed at about 11 o'clock this evening.
Vi reiser til Norge til høsten.	We will travel to Norway this fall.
I morgen blir det snø.	It will snow tomorrow.
Snart ringer vi ham.	We'll call him soon.

Continuing action

Han sitter og skriver brev.	He is writing [sitting and writing] letters.
Tone går og tenker.	Tone is thinking [walking and thinking].
Mannen står og koper på dem.	The man is staring [standing and staring] at them.
Karin ligger og leser avisa.	Karin is reading [lying and reading] the newspaper.

7 Modal Helping Verbs

Modal helping verbs (like English *will* or *must*) express modes or conditions. In Norwegian they are used to describe future, desired, recommended, allowed, or conditional events. Unlike English, these modal forms can appear in the infinitive, present, past, and perfect tenses. In Norwegian it is possible to have two or more modal verbs in a row: **Må jeg ville kunne snakke norsk?** "Do I need to want to be able to speak Norwegian?" While the perfect forms exist for all of these modals, several are rarely used.

The grammatical form of past tense for the modal does not always imply a past event. These modal helping verbs can be used to make a statement or request less direct and more polite than the corresponding phrases. The past tenses **kunne, skulle,** and **ville** also reduce the abruptness of certain requests:

Sett deg.	Sit down.
Kan du sette deg?	Can you sit down?
Vil du sette deg?	Will you sit down?
Kunne du sette deg?	Could you sit down?

The main verb, the one that follows these helping verbs, must always be in the infinitive without the infinitive marker **å,** though it may also be left off when it describes movement toward a specific goal. This holds for the modals **måtte, skulle,** and **ville.**

Vi skal reise til Moskva.   We will travel to Moscow.
or
Vi skal til Moskva.

Jeg må gå hjem nå. or **Jeg må hjem nå.**	I have to go home now.

The main verb can also be omitted in certain questions using modals:

Hva må du gjøre? or **Hva må du?**	What do you need to do?
Hvorfor skal du gjøre det? or **Hvorfor skal du det?**	Why will you do that?

Common Modal Verbs

Burde: **å burde, bør, burde, har burdet**   ought to, should

Dere bør sitte stille en stund.	You (plural) ought to sit quietly a while.
Han burde ha gjort hjemmeleksene nøyere.	He ought to have done his homework more accurately.
Vi har burdet skrive brev til våre venner.	We should have written to our friends.

Få: **å få, får, fikk, har fått**   have permission to, need to, cause to

The verb **å få** is considered a modal in some of its many functions. As a main verb, **få** means "get, receive," but as a modal it can mean "have permission to, be able to, need to, cause to, manage to."

Så skulle hun få mannen sin til å gjøre det.	Then she could get her husband to do it.
Vi får se om David greier seg.	We'll see if David manages it.
De fikk reise til slutt.	They got to go finally.
Jeg er så glad for å ha fått se dem.	I am so happy I have managed to see them.

Forfatteren fikk solgt bokmanuset til et stort forlag.	The author managed to sell the book manuscript to a big publisher.

Kunne: **å kunne, kan, kunne, har kunnet**   can, be able to

Karin ville kunne snakke arabisk.	Karin wanted to be able to speak Arabic.
Kan du svømme godt?	Can you swim well?
Vi forklarte hvordan en slik bevegelse kunne slå rot i Norge.	We explained how such a movement could take root in Norway.
Til nå, har jeg ikke kunnet forstå min venn.	Until now, I was not able to understand my friend.

Måtte: **å måtte, må, måtte, har måttet**   have to, must

Jeg må spise fordi jeg er sulten.	I have to eat because I'm hungry.
Å måtte skrive nynorsk er noe mange unge nordmenn misliker.	To have to write Nynorsk is something many young Norwegians dislike.
Det betyr at han må kjempe hardere.	That means he has to fight harder.
Klara måtte bli hjemme fordi hun ikke hadde skrevet ferdig essayet.	Klara had to stay home because she hadn't finished writing her essay.
Jeg har måttet arbeide på fabrikk de to siste åra.	I had to work in a factory for the last two years.

Skulle: å skulle, skal, skulle, har skullet   shall, will

See the comments on the use of **skulle** for future events and with the conditional.

Det er viktig å skulle tenke om framtida.	It is important to think about the future.
Hvilket mål—bokmål eller nynorsk—skal brukes her?	Which form—Bokmål or Nynorsk—will be used here?
Han skulle ha gjort leksene før.	He should have done his lessons previously.
Dere har skullet vært til stede.	You should have been present.

Tore: å tore, tør, torde, har tort   dare to

Den unge jenta tør ikke gå på høyloftet i mørket selv.	The young girl dares not go alone to the hayloft in the dark.
Få i byen torde protestere mot naziestene.	Few in town dared protest against the Nazis.

Ville: å ville, vil, ville, har villet   want, will

See the comments on the use of **vil** for future events.

Per må ville gjøre det, ellers blir ingenting gjort.	Per has to want to do it; otherwise nothing will be done.
Jeg vil verken svare ja eller nei på det spørsmålet.	I will not (or do not want to) answer either yes or no to that question.
Da de skulle seile, ville gutten ikke være med.	When they were about to sail, the boy did not want to go along.
Jeg har aldri villet tro at moren var død.	I have never wanted to believe that mother was dead.

8 Forms of the Past Tense

Past tense and past participle forms of Norwegian verbs fall into two large categories—regular and irregular—which may then be subdivided further. The four classes of regular past tense verbs are discussed below, as are the verbs with irregular past forms. Verbs with irregular present forms do not necessarily also have irregular past forms (e.g., **ville, vil, ville, har villet**). The forms of many regular and irregular Norwegian verbs are listed alphabetically in the appendix beginning on page 137.

Regular Verbs

Regular past tense verbs (sometimes called "weak" verbs) are those that maintain the same vowel in the stem of the verb but add an ending with **-d** or **-t**. Each of the four classes of regular verbs in Norwegian uses different endings with **-d** or **-t** that are partially predictable according to the structure of the verb's stem.

English makes the same distinction between regular and irregular verbs. All regular verbs in English add *-ed* to the verb stem to form the past tense (for example *to play* ⇔ *played*). Note that the verb *to give* ⇔ *gave* in English is strong, because the vowel in the infinitive alternates with the vowel in the past tense (*i* ⇔ *a*).

A few verbs have alternative forms in several classes, stemming from dialectal differences. These alternative forms are accommodated in today's *Bokmål*. For example **å klage** "to complain" can have the past tense **klaget** (Class I) or **klagde** (Class III). Some strong verbs end in **-t** or **-d** but are considered strong because the stem vowel varies between infinitive and past tense forms. For example, notice the vowel difference in **å gjøre** "to do" and **gjorde** "did."

Class I

A very large group of Norwegian regular verbs fall into this group. They add **-et** to the stem form. Many verbs have a double consonant ending in their stems. There is an alternative ending **-a** for past tense in this class. **Han åpnet/åpna døra** "He opened the door." While the ending **-a** is allowed in *Bokmål,* it is much rarer than the **-et** endings that are presented below.

Infinitive	Past Tense	English
å snakke	snakket/snakka	to speak, spoke
å danse	danset/dansa	to dance, danced
å vente	ventet/venta	to wait, waited

Class II

The other fairly large class of weak verbs adds **-te** to the verb's stem to form the past tense. For the most part, the infinitive has a long vowel followed by only one consonant. A few clear examples are:

Infinitive	Past Tense	English
å kjøpe	kjøpte	to buy, bought
å låne	lånte	to borrow/lend borrowed/lent
å reise	reiste	to travel, traveled
å spise	spiste	eat, ate

A few consonant clusters (groups of consonants) function as a single consonant and are thus included among Class II regular verbs. Stems with **-nd** and **-ld** for example are included here, as are the verbs with these double consonants in their stems: **ll, mm,** and **nn.** Double consonants are most often simplified (see chapter 4). The chart below gives one example of each cluster.

Infinitive	Past Tense	English
å bestemme	bestemte	to decide, decided
å kalle	kalte	to call, called
å kjenne	kjente	to know (a person), knew
å melde	meldte	to report, reported
å sende	sendte	to send, sent

Class III

For this class, the past tense ending -de is added to the stem. These verbs generally have stems that end in a diphthong (for example ei), or in a -g or -v.

Infinitive	Past Tense	English
å greie	greide	to manage, managed
å klage	klagde/klaget/klaga	to complain, complained
å prøve	prøvde	to try, tried

Class IV

Verbs in this class have past tenses that end in -dde. Generally verbs with stems that end in stressed vowels fall into Class IV; the stem (to which the -dde is added) is equivalent to the infinitive.

Infinitive	Past Tense	English
å bo	bodde	to live, lived
å nå	nådde	to reach, reached
å tro	trodde	to believe, believed

Irregular Verbs

Many of the most common verbs in Norwegian have irregular forms for the past tense. There is generally no way to guess what the form is, so memorization or consulting lists is important. Strong verbs are those that alternate stem vowels in the infinitive, present, and past tense. A good example in English of a strong verb is *drive* (infinitive) and *drove* (past tense). While patterns do exist for these verbs, it is probably easier to learn the forms through use and repetition rather than through analytical classifications. Norwegian strong verbs are very commonly used, so the student will have plenty of opportunity to practice them. Alternate forms that Norwegian students may use in writing, but that are not standard in textbooks, are given in brackets—as is the tradition in Norwegian word lists.

Infinitive	Past Tense	English
å bli	ble/blei/vart	to become, became
å bære	bar	to bear, bore
å drikke	drakk	to drink, drank
å finne	fant	to find, found
å få	fikk [fekk]	to get, got
å gi	gav [ga]	to give, gave
å gjøre	gjorde	to do, did
å gå	gikk [gjekk]	to go, went
å hjelpe	hjalp	to help, helped
å ligge	lå	to lie, lay
å si	sa	to say, said
å sitte	satt	to sit, sat
å skrive	skrev/skreiv	to write, wrote
å sove	sov	to sleep, slept
å spørre	spurte	to ask, asked

å stå	stod [sto]	to stand, stood
å ta	tok	to take, took
å treffe	traff	to meet, met
å vite	visste	to know, knew
å være	var	to be, was/were

A more complete list of strong and regular verbs, giving past tense and past participle, appears in chapter 9.

Examples of Past Tense Use

The past tense is used to describe events that began and ended at a specific time in the past. It can also describe events that occurred often or repeatedly in the past. In addition, a speaker can use this tense to express an immediate sensation or opinion. In this case, the statement refers to the present.

Specific past time

Egil var i Bergen for en uke siden.	Egil was in Bergen a week ago.
Besøkte dere familien deres i fjor?	Did you all visit your family last year?
Barna skrev mange brev til besteforeldrene.	The children wrote many letters to their grandparents.
Andersson bodde i Tromsø i 1995.	Andersson lived in Tromsø in 1995.
Bombardementet begynte lørdag.	The bombing began on Saturday.

Repeated past actions

Karin kjørte til hytta tre ganger om uken.	Karin drove to the cabin three times a week.
Farfar fortalte ofte om det gamle landet.	Grandfather often told of the old country.

Description of present sensation

The past tense in this case describes a reaction to or description of a present sensation.

Det var hyggelig å treffe deg!   It is nice to meet you!

Kaken var deilig.   The cake is delicious.

9 Present Perfect and Past Perfect Tenses

The present perfect tense describes events that have taken place at an indeterminate time before the utterance or that have lasted for an indeterminate length of time. Since it does not matter exactly when the activity has taken place (other than at some point in the past), the main focus is on the outcome and consequence of the action. The past tense, on the other hand, is used for events that occurred at specific, named times in the past.

The present perfect is formed with the present form of an auxiliary verb, either **har** "have, has" or **er** "am, is, are" together with the past participle. It is always correct to use **har,** but Norwegians may also use **er** as the auxiliary. The use of **er** is more restricted, and generally with verbs of motion or state. Usage may be somewhat determined by regional dialect, with Northern and Western dialects favoring **er,** and **har** more common elsewhere; convention suggests using **er** when highlighting the end result and using **har** when the focus is on the action itself. Historical and formal documents tend to use **er** with verbs of motion and **har** with all others.

Har du lest boken om Sofie?	Have you read the book about Sofie?
Framtida er alt kommet.	The future has already arrived.
Boka ble forbudt straks den var kommet ut.	The book was forbidden as soon as it was published.
Det har aldri kommet en revolusjon i Norge.	There has never been a revolution in Norway.
Det er et ord som må være kommet inn med hanseatene.	It is a word that must have entered with the Hanseatic traders.

The Past Participle

The past participle in Norwegian generally follows a pattern similar to the past tense form (see appendix beginning on page 137) with endings in **-t** or **-d.** Only a few strong verb past participles end in **-d;** the vast majority end in **-t.**

A few verbs have alternative forms in several classes. For example, **å klage** "to complain" can have the past participle **klaget** (Class II) or **klagd** (Class IV). Some strong verbs have the typical weak verb **-t** or **-d** ending but are considered strong because the stem vowel varies between infinitive and past tense forms.

In addition to its use in forming the present and past perfect, the past participle is also used in the passive construction and as an adjective (see chapters 13 and 18).

Regular Verbs

Class I

This large class of weak verbs adds **-et** to the stem to form the past participle. Many verbs have a stem-final double consonant or consonant cluster. There is an alternative ending for past participle **-a** in this class. **Han har åpnet/har åpna vinduet** "He has opened the window." While the ending **-a** is allowed in *Bokmål,* it is much rarer than **-et** endings and should be avoided by students.

Infinitive	Present Perfect	English
å snakke	har snakket/snakka	to speak; have, has spoken
å danse	har danset/dansa	to dance; have, has danced
å vente	har ventet/venta	to wait; have, has waited

Class II

A very large percentage of Norwegian regular verbs fall into this group. Verbs in this class add **-t** to form the past perfect. For the most part, the infinitive has a long vowel followed by only one consonant. A few clear examples are:

Infinitive	Present Perfect	English
å kjøpe	har kjøpt	to buy; have, has bought

å låne	har lånt	to borrow/lend; have, has borrowed/lent
å reise	har reist	to travel; have, has traveled
å spise	har spist	eat; have, has eaten

A few stem-final consonant clusters function as single consonants and are thus grouped with Class II regular verbs. Stems with **-nd** and **-ld** are included here, as are the verbs with the double consonants **-ll, -mm,** and **-nn** in their stems. Stem-final double consonants are simplified with the addition of endings (see chapter 4). The chart below gives one example of each cluster.

Infinitive	Past Participle	English
å bestemme	har bestemt	to decide; have, has decided
å kalle	har kalt	to call; have, has called
å kjenne	har kjent	to know (a person); have, has known
å melde	har meldt	to report; have, has reported
å sende	har sendt	to send; have, has sent

Class III

The past participle ending in Class III, **-d,** is added to the stem. Verbs in this class generally have stems that end in a diphthong, **-g,** or **-v.**

Infinitive	Present Perfect	English
å greie	har greid	to manage; have, has managed
å klage	har klagd/klaget/klaga	to complain; have, has complained

Class IV

Weak verbs in this class have past participles that add **-dd** to the stem (and to the infinitive). Generally, verbs with stems that end in stressed vowels fall into this class.

Infinitive	Present Perfect	English
å bo	har bodd	to live; have, has lived
å nå	har nådd	to reach; have, has reached
å tro	har trodd	to believe; have, has believed

Irregular Verbs

Many of the most common verbs in Norwegian have irregular forms in the past participle. There is generally no way to guess what the form is, so memorization or consulting lists is important. Strong verbs are verbs that alternate stem vowels in the infinitive (and present tense) and in the past tense. A good English example of a strong verb is *drink* (infinitive) and *drunk* (past participle). While patterns do exist for these verbs, it is probably easier to learn the forms through use and repetition rather than through analytical classifications. Norwegian strong verbs are very commonly used, so the student will have plenty of opportunity to practice them. Some of the most common irregular verbs are listed below:

Infinitive	Present Perfect	English
å bli	har blitt	to become; have, has become
å bære	har båret	to bear; have, has borne
å drikke	har drukket	to drink; have, has drunk
å finne	har funnet	to find; have, has found
å få	har fått	to get; have, has gotten
å gi	har gitt	to give; have, has given

å gjøre	har gjort	to do; have, has done
å gå	har gått	to go; have, has gone
å hjelpe	har hjulpet	to help; have, has helped
å ligge	har ligget	to lie; have, has lain
å si	har sagt	to say; have, has said
å sitte	har sittet	to sit; have, has sat
å skrive	har skrevet	to write; have, has written
å sove	har sovet	to sleep; have, has slept
å spørre	har spurt	to ask; have, has asked
å stå	har stått	to stand; have, has stood
å ta	har tatt	to take; have, has taken
å treffe	har truffet	to meet; have, has met
å vite	har visst	to know; have, has known
å være	har vært	to be; have, has been

A complete list of 225 verbs, including past tense and past participle forms, appears in the appendix beginning on page 137.

Examples of Present Perfect Use

Jeg har aldri sett et ansikt som ditt.	I have never seen a face like yours.
Vi har vært gift i fem år nå.	We've been married for five years now.
Senere har han fortalt om hvor fascinert han ble av henne.	Later he told about how fascinated he was with her.
Familien hans har brutt kontakten med ham.	His family has broken off contact with him.

Man har ofte sagt at språkene er menneskehetens vinduer mot virkeligheten.	People have often said that languages are humanity's windows on reality.

Past Perfect

The past perfect denotes that an event in the past took place before another named event. The earlier event uses the past perfect, while the more recent one uses the past tense. The past perfect uses an auxiliary verb (most often **hadde** "had," sometimes **var** "was") with the past participle.

Jeg dro ned til sentrum etter at jeg hadde spist lunsj.	I went downtown after I had eaten lunch.
Etter at jeg hadde lært norsk, studerte jeg norrønt.	After I had learned Norwegian, I studied Old Norse.
Jeg hadde kokt kaffe før mannen kom.	I had made coffee before the man arrived.

10 Participles

Present Participles Used as Adjectives

Participles are adjective forms based on verbs, and may be used in a variety of ways in English and Norwegian. English uses the present participle (the *-ing* form) in the so-called progressive tenses, which describe activities that extend over a period of time.

I am thinking.

She was dreaming.

Olav had been playing tennis.

Norwegian has no corresponding verbal usage of present participles. Present participles are used as adjectives, describing nouns, or pronouns. To form the present participle, Norwegian adds **-ende** to the stem.

Infinitive	Present Participle	English
å sove	sovende	sleeping
å leke	lekende	playing
å dominere	dominerende	dominant, dominating
å stå	stående	standing

Norges dominerende skriftspråk er bokmål.	Norway's dominant written form is Bokmål.

Videregående skoler gir utdanning utover grunnskolen.	High schools (continuing schools) give training beyond elementary school.
Det smilende barnet bare satt stille.	The smiling child just sat quietly.
Svar på følgende spørsmål.	Answer the following questions.
Ikke et levende sjel var tilstede.	Not a living soul was present.
Nyhetene er også sjokkerende for oss.	The news is also shocking for us.
Prøv vår imponerende database.	Try our impressive (= impressing) database.
Den utøvende makt er hos Kongen, eller hos Dronningen hvis hun har ervervet kronen.	The executive power rests with the King, or with the Queen if she has acceded to the throne (acquired the crown).

Participial adjectives are often used as nouns:

Si nei til guruer, allvitende, og metoder.	Say no to gurus, know-it-alls, and methods.
De nynorsktallende er en minoritet på Østlandet.	Nynorsk speakers (= Nynorsk-speaking people) are a minority in eastern Norway.
Du må henvende deg til rette vedkommende.	You must address yourself to the proper authorities.

Adverbs can be formed from the neuter form of adjectives. Since adjectives that end in **-ende** do not take special neuter endings, all present participial adjectives are also adverbs:

Han kom løpende.	He came running.
Hunden stirret granskende på meg.	The dog stared searchingly at me.
Læreren skottet spørrende bort på meg.	The teacher glanced questioningly over at me.

The present participle is often combined with a form of **å bli** and followed by an infinitive to express a continuing action:

Han ble sittende og prate.	He remained sitting and chatted.
De ble stående og måpe.	They remained standing and stared.

Past Participles Used as Adjectives

In addition to their use in forming the perfect tenses and the passive, past participles also have an important function as adjectives:

De undertrykte er ikke hjelpeløse.	The oppressed are not helpless.
Han prøvde å sprenge de gitte betingelsene for livet sitt.	He tried to break open the given constraints on his life.
Undertegnede er prosjektleder.	The undersigned is the project leader.

When used as adjectives, past participles are given endings to agree with the noun they modify. Weak verbs that have participles in **-et** can use either **-ede** or **-ete** forms in the definite or plural.

Bortkastet "thrown away," the past participial adjective related to the verb **å kaste bort** (**å bortkaste**), has the following forms:

en bortkastet bil	an abandoned car; a thrown-away car
et bortkastet hefte	a thrown-away notebook
mange bortkastede/bortkastete timer	many wasted hours

The following are additional examples of weak verb past participle forms:

det smeltede blyet	the smelted lead
gamle hvitstammede bjerker	old white-trunked birch trees
hans forstyrrede tankegang	his disturbed thought process

Strong verbs that have past participles ending in **-et** use forms ending in **-ne** when the adjectives are in the definite or plural form:

den vidåpne ovnsdøren	the wide-open oven door
mange velskrevne bøker	many well-written books

But when these adjectives are used in the predicate (with a verb separating the adjective from the noun), the form ends in **-et** (the neuter form of the participle):

Ovnsdøren er vidåpnet.	The oven door is wide open.
Bøkene er velskrevet.	The books are well written.

11 Future Tense

Future activities in Norwegian are not expressed with a special tense as they are in other languages such as French. Rather, like English, Norwegian uses several methods to show and describe coming events.

Helping Verbs Skal and Vil

Use of a modal helping verb combined with the infinitive is the most common way to indicate futurity. **Skal** and **vil** are used the most. **Skal** "shall" is used when the speaker intends to undertake the activity and maintains control over the decisions and plans. The event has been planned. **Vil** "will" expresses an event in which the speaker is involved, but over which he has no control. **Vil** is used less often than **skal** to express the future. English speakers need to guard against overuse of **vil,** especially where they would use "will" in an equivalent English sentence. In Norwegian **vil** most often expresses "want to" or "it is my will to."

Vi skal vaske bilen i morgen.	We shall/will wash the car tomorrow.
Vi vil vaske bilen i morgen.	We want to wash the car tomorrow.
Jeg skal bli forfatter.	I'm going to be an author.
Skal vi forsøke å ringe foreldrene dine?	Shall we try to call your parents?
Jeg håper at denne boken vil bli brukt av mange folk.	I hope that this book will be used by many people.

Når man skal skrive om et emne som dette, er det viktig å lese alle kildene.	When one is going to write about a subject like this, it is important to read all the sources.

The Idiom Kommer til å

Using the idiomatic expression **kommer til å** + infinitive is a common way to denote a future event. It is very similar to the English "going to." Use of the expression suggests that the event is anywhere from moderately likely to absolutely likely to occur. This expression has an informal tone to it.

Vi kommer til å reise i morgen.	We are going to leave tomorrow.
Ann kommer til å gjøre det snart.	Ann will do it soon.
Det kommer vel til å regne i morgen.	I suppose it'll rain tomorrow.
Bente kommer til å ringe deg i kveld.	Bente is going to call you this evening.
Det kommer til å bli enda verre neste måned.	It's going to get even worse next month.
Noen lingvister mener at omtrent halvparten av språkene kommer til å forsvinne før året 2100.	Some linguists think that about half of the languages are going to disappear before the year 2100.

Present Tense

Events that will take place in the future are very often expressed with a present tense verb. The future aspect is referenced generally with an adverb (**snart** "soon") or adverbial phrase (**i morgen** "tomorrow" or **om en uke** "in a week").

Vi begynner om en time.	We will begin in an hour.
Kommer du snart på besøk?	Are you coming to visit soon?
Wenche kjøper hus til høsten.	Wenche will buy a house next fall.

På lørdag spiser vi hos dem.	On Saturday, we'll eat at their place.
Når går flyet?	When will the plane leave?
Lisbet bestiller teaterbillettene seinere.	Lisbet will order the theater tickets later.

12 Conditionals and Subjunctives

Norwegian, unlike French and German, does not have specific "ready-made" grammatical forms for expressing "what if" situations. Rather, it uses verbal phrases with helping verbs (see also chapter 7). English and Norwegian are similar in their use of these constructions.

Conditional

To express statements of desire, or wishes that may be contrary to known facts, Norwegian uses the modal helping verb **skulle** "should." Expressions using **skulle** may describe a future event, as seen from a distinct point in the past.

I går skulle hun gå på kino.	Yesterday, she was going to go to the movies.
Han skulle komme om en time.	He was going to arrive in an hour.
Hovedformene skulle brukes i lærebøker.	The main forms should be/are supposed to be used in textbooks.
Nittenåttiåtte skulle bli det året han skrev sitt første fullførte teaterstykke.	Nineteen eighty-eight was supposed to be the year he wrote his first complete play.
Moren skulle kjøre til Oslo.	Mother was going to drive to Oslo.

For conditional statements of events in the past, Norwegians often omit the auxiliary verb **ha.**

48

| Han skulle ha skrevet til oss før. ⇒ **Han skulle skrevet til oss før.** | He should have written us before. |

Subordinate Clauses

Conditions can be stated in subordinate clauses beginning with **hvis** "if," **om** "whether," or **dersom** "if":

Vi ville reise til Norge hvis vi hadde råd.	We would go to Norway if we could afford it.
Det hadde vært hyggelig om du kunne skrive noen ord.	It would have been nice if you could have dropped me a line (written a couple of words).
Om vi kunne velge et av de nordiske språkene, ville det bli bokmålet.	If we could choose one of the Nordic languages, it would be Bokmål.

Without using a specific word, Norwegian can indicate the conditional aspect of a clause by inverting verb-subject order. This can be done in English as well but is rare: "Had I known then what I know now. . . ."

| **Hadde jeg tenkt på det tidligere, ville jeg ha gjort det.** | If I had thought about it earlier/Had I thought about it earlier, I would have done it. |

For more explanation of conjunctions and subordinate clauses, see chapter 23.

Subjunctive

While French, German, and many other languages have special grammatical forms for the subjunctive mode, subjunctive forms in Norwegian are rare, and limited to several frozen expressions. The form used is the same as the infinitive. The subjunctive expresses wishes or contrary-to-fact conditions.

| **Leve kongen!** | Long live the king! |
| **Gud bevare oss.** | God save us. |

13 Passives

Sentences (and their verb forms) can be either active or passive, depending on the point of view of the speaker or writer. When the focus is on the action and its doer, we use the active voice. When the focus is on the object being acted upon rather than the doer—or subject—then we use the passive voice.

Active

In active sentences, the verb expresses an action that has an effect or impact on the object. The subject performs the action. Most sentences in normal speech and writing are active. The following sentences use the active voice:

Eivind leste boka. Eivind read the book.

Russerne skilte mennene fra kvinner og barn. The Russians separated the men from the women and children.

Passive

In passive sentences the central focus rests on the action itself and the person or thing that is acted upon. The English passive construction uses the verb *to be* and the past participle: *The cake was eaten. The batter was beaten. The mouse is being chased (by the cat).*

Norwegian forms passives in two ways: the **bli** passive and the **-s** passive.

1   Bli passive construction

Bli passives use a form of the verb **bli** (**å bli, blir, ble/blei, har blitt**) and the past participle of the main verb. Compare the active and passive forms below:

Katten spiser fisken.   The cat is eating the fish.

In this active construction the subject (cat) is doing the action (is eating) to the object (the fish).

Fisken blir spist (av katten).   The fish is being eaten
                                             (by the cat).

In the related passive sentence, the fish (and the eating) is the focal point—the cat need not be mentioned at all. When the logical subject is mentioned, it is introduced by the Norwegian preposition **av**.

The tense of **bli** matches the tense of the main verb in the corresponding active sentence:

Tense	Active	Bli passive
Infinitive	**å spise** to eat	**å bli spist** to be eaten
Present	**spiser** eats	**blir spist** is (being) eaten
Past	**spiste** ate	**ble spist** was (being) eaten
Conditional	**skulle/ville spise** would eat	**skulle/ville bli spist** would be eaten
Future	**skal spise** shall eat	**skal bli spist** shall be eaten
Future perfect	**skal ha spist** shall have eaten	**skal ha blitt spist** shall have been eaten
Present perfect	**har spist** has eaten	**har blitt spist** has been eaten
Past perfect	**hadde spist** had eaten	**hadde blitt spist** had been eaten

The following examples show use of the **bli** passive:

De ble ført bort til ukjent sted.	They were led away to an undisclosed location.
Tre mennesker hadde blitt drept.	Three people had been killed.
Tittelen har blitt endret.	The title has been changed.
Hovedrollen blir spilt av Liv Ullmann.	The main role is played by Liv Ullmann.
Det blir begått et mord i romanen.	A murder was committed in the novel.

2   -s passive construction

In addition to the **bli** passive, Norwegians can use another type known as the **-s** passive. This passive construction is more limited in use stylistically, and less extensive in its forms. To form verbs in the **-s** passive, an **-s** is added to the infinitive form of the verb.

While specific events are usually described using the **bli** passive, the **-s** passive is used in describing events that are ongoing or general. **-s** passives are common after modal helping verbs: **må spises** "must be eaten," **kan spises** "can be eaten," and **måtte spises** "had to be eaten." Other **-s** passive constructions tend to sound bookish or administrative.

Tense	Active	-s passive
Infinitive	**å spise** to eat	**å spises** to be eaten
Present	**spiser** eats	**spises** is (being) eaten
Past	**spiste** ate	—
Conditional	**skulle/ville spise** should eat	**skulle/ville spises** would be eaten
Future	**skal spise** shall eat	**skal spises** shall be eaten
Future perfect	**skal ha spist** shall have eaten	—

Present perfect   **har spist** has eaten   —

Past perfect   **hadde spist** had eaten   —

The following are examples of **-s** passive:

Aslaug må undersøkes av barnelegen.	Aslaug needs to be examined by the pediatrician.
Vi kan ikke påvirkes av noe eller noen utenfor oss.	We cannot be influenced by anything or anyone outside of ourselves.
Forfatteren argumenterer her for at inflasjon skapes av myndighetene.	The author argues here that inflation is created by the authorities.

14 -s Verbs

While most Norwegian verbs end in **-r** or **-er** in the present tense (e.g., **har** "has," **anbefaler** "recommends"), several important verb classes have an **-s** ending.

-s Passive

The so-called **-s** passive can be used in the present tense and the infinitive, and is discussed extensively in the previous chapter.

Active Verbs with -s Forms

A small number of Norwegian verbs have active meanings, but end with **-s** and look like passive forms. Sometimes called "deponent verbs," they have infinitive, present, and past forms ending in **-s.** The past participle form is rarely used.

Infinitive	Present tense	Past tense	Present perfect	English
å finnes	**finnes/fins**	**fantes/fans**	**har funnes**	to be found, exist
å følges	**følges**	**fulgtes**	**har fulgtes**	to be followed, to succeed
å kjennes	**kjennes**	**kjentes**	**har kjentes**	to perceive
å lykkes	**lykkes**	**lyktes**	**har lykkes**	to succeed

å minnes	minnes	mintes	har mintes	remember, recall
å synes	synes/syns	syntes	har synes/ har syns	to seem, to think
å trives	trives	trivdes	har trives/ har trivs	to thrive, to enjoy
å undres	undres	undredes	har undres	to wonder about, ponder
å spørres	spørs	spurtes	har spurts	depends on, is a question of

Hva synes du om filmen?	What do you think of the movie?
Vinden syntes å ha gått til hvile.	The wind seemed to have gone to sleep.
De fleste legere synes å være enige om at det er en farlig sykdom.	Most doctors seem to agree that this is a dangerous disease.
En voldsom folkemasse samles på torget.	A violent crowd is gathering in the marketplace.
Vi trivdes svært godt i Bodø.	We enjoyed ourselves very much in Bodø.
Deres salgssuksesser kunne ikke følges opp med nye opplag.	Their sales successes could not be followed up with new editions.
Forslaget høres utmerket ut.	The suggestion sounds excellent.
Det spørs om han kommer.	It depends on whether he comes.

Reciprocal Verbs

Reciprocal verbs, which also end in **-s,** express how the subjects of a sentence interact.

Infinitive	Present tense	Past tense	Present perfect	English
å møtes	møtes	møttes	har møttes	to meet each other
å omgås/ omgåes	omgås/ omgåes	omgikks	har omgåts/ har omgåttes	to associate with, pass without noticing each other
å ses/å sees	ses/sees	sås/såes	har ses/ har sees (rare)	to see each other
å skilles	skilles	skiltes	har skiltes	to separate, to be divorced
å slåss	slåss	sloss	har slåss	to fight

Vi har møttes bare to ganger tidligere.	We have met each other only two times before.
Mannen og kvinnen omgikks på gata.	The man and woman passed each other on the street.
I et slikt miljø må man lære seg å omgås andre på en smidig måte.	In this kind of milieu, one needs to learn to associate with others in a flexible manner.
Jeg håper vi skilles som gode venner.	I hope we separate as good friends.
Ha det! Vi sees om en uke.	Bye! I'll see you (we'll see each other) in a week.

Part Two

Essentials of Norwegian Grammar

15 Nouns

Nouns are names that refer to people, places, physical objects, concepts, and actions.

Gender

In Norwegian, nouns fall into one of three grammatical classes or *genders.* The three genders are sometimes referred to as *masculine, feminine,* and *neuter,* although this classification has little to do with natural genders. Because there is no obvious connection between nouns and their gender, students must either memorize or look up genders to use the correct forms. Approximately 55 percent of all Norwegian nouns are masculine, 25 percent neuter gender, and 20 percent feminine.

Masculine nouns are often called **en** nouns because their indefinite article is **en.** Similarly, feminine nouns are **ei** nouns and neuters **et.** Almost all **ei** nouns can be considered **en** nouns, and use **en** forms as alternates. Thinking of **ei** nouns as a subset of **en** nouns may perhaps be helpful.

Number

Nouns can be either singular or plural. Some nouns represent objects that can be counted (like **eple** "apple"), while others represent non-countables (**melk** "milk"). Non-countable nouns can be called "mass nouns," and generally do not have plural forms.

Indefinite and Definite Forms

A noun is usually in the indefinite when it is introduced into conversation or writing. The noun represents something unspecified, not differentiated from all the other items of its sort. English uses the indefinite singular article "a" or "an," which, since English does not have grammatical gender, is used for all nouns. Norwegian indefinite articles vary according to the gender of the noun, as noted above. In neither language are articles used with indefinite plurals.

The definite article is used to indicate a specific noun or a noun that has been referred to previously. Here English uses the free-standing definite article **the,** while Norwegian uses a suffix. The specific form of the suffix depends on gender and number. The text that follows shows the most general pattern for **en, ei,** and **et** nouns in all four forms (indefinite singular, definite singular, indefinite plural, definite plural). When suffixes are added, the unstressed -**e** ending on the noun is removed first. For example, the definite singular ending -**a** for **ei jente** "a girl" is added to **jent-: jenta** "the girl."

Uses of Indefinite and Definite Forms

Definite forms of nouns are used generally when the noun under discussion has been introduced previously, or when there is only one such item and no additional modifier is needed to understand the reference (for example **månen** "the moon"). In the following examples, Norwegian—unlike English—uses the definite forms.

1. Possessive constructions with the "owner" named after the noun:

   huset mitt   my house

   bilen til Janne   Janne's car

2. Demonstrative constructions (although there can be variation):

   denne bilen   this car

   de barna   those children

3. Some set phrases with specific meanings require definite forms:

   om vinteren   during the winter

   til høsten   this coming fall

   heile natta   the whole night

   halve kongeriket   half the kingdom

4. Abstract nouns:

Slik er livet.   Such is life.

Naturen i Norge er vidunderlig.   The landscape, the scenery
                                           (nature) in Norway
                                           is wonderful.

5. Body parts (used without a possessive):

Jeg har vondt i hodet.   I have a headache.
                                           (*lit.* I have bad in the head.)

Han tok meg i hånden.   He held my hand.

6. Quantity per units (e.g., $5 a pound)

Det koster kr 20 kiloen.   It costs 20 kroner a
                                           (*lit.* = the) kilo.

Jeg kjørte 100 km timen.   I drove 100 kilometers an
                                           (*lit.* = the) hour.

The following are cases in which Norwegian does not use the indefinite article.
Equivalent phrases in English use **a** or **an.**

1. Professions, nationalities, and religions:

Hun er sykerpleier.   She is a nurse.

Tom er nordmann.   Tom is a Norwegian.

Sham er muslim.   Sham is a Muslim.

2. Focus on general activity uses the noun without an article:

Kåre liker å kjøre bil.   Kåre likes car driving
                                           (to car-drive).

Jeg skriver brev i ettermiddag.   I am letter writing this
                                           afternoon.

When the profession, nationality, or activity is further specified, Norwegian uses an indefinite article:

Hun er en fin sykepleier.   She is a fine nurse.

Jeg skriver et langt brev i ettermiddag.   I am writing a long letter this afternoon.

En Nouns

Singular		Plural	
Indefinite	**Definite**	**Indefinite**	**Definite**
en —	add -**en**	add -**er**	add -**ene**
en bil a car	**bilen** the car	**biler** cars	**bilene** the cars
en stol a chair	**stolen** the chair	**stoler** chairs	**stolene** the chairs
en radio a radio	**radioen** the radio	**radioer** radios	**radioene** the radios
en vei a road	**veien** the road	**veier** roads	**veiene** the roads
en følelse a feeling	**følelsen** the feeling	**følelser** feelings	**følelsene** the feelings

Ei Nouns

Feminine nouns (**ei** nouns) hold a special position in Norwegian grammar. The nouns in the class can, for the most part, also be **en** nouns (the converse is not true). In certain situations, a speaker may prefer the feminine form, while that same person in other situations will use the masculine form. In formal settings, speakers are more likely to use masculine forms, whereas casual, informal, peer-to-peer dialectal speech favors liberal use of feminine forms. For a few nouns, the use of the feminine is mandated, both by convention and by the *Språkråd* (Norwegian Language Council). These nouns are marked with asterisks below. For all other feminine nouns, official orthographic lists count the masculine and feminine as equal principal forms.

Singular		Plural	
Indefinite	**Definite**	**Indefinite**	**Definite**
ei —	add **-a**	add **-er**	add **-ene**
* **ei jente** a girl	**jenta** the girl	**jenter** girls	**jentene** the girls
* **ei ku** a cow	**kua** the cow	**kuer** cows	**kuene** the cows
* **ei fele** a fiddle	**fela** the fiddle	**feler** fiddles	**felene** the fiddles
* **ei geit** a goat	**geita** the goat	**geiter** goats	**geitene** the goats
ei kone a wife	**kona** the wife	**koner** wives	**konene** the wives
ei klokke a clock	**klokka** the clock	**klokker** clocks	**klokkene** the clocks
ei utgreiing a report	**utgreiinga** the report	**utgreiinger** reports	**utgreiingene** the report
ei tante an aunt	**tanta** the aunt	**tanter** aunts	**tantene** the aunts

Et Nouns

Neuter nouns differ in a number of ways from **en** and **ei** nouns. Most one-syllable **et** nouns and several **et** nouns with more than one syllable do not have an **-r** ending in the indefinite plural (e.g., **et hus—mange hus**). In addition, many **et** nouns allow—but do not require—an **-a** ending in the definite plural form.

Singular		Plural	
Indefinite	**Definite**	**Indefinite**	**Definite**
et —	add **-et**	add — or **-er**	add **-a** or **-ene**
et år a year	**året** the year	**år** years	**årene/åra** the years
et bilde a picture	**bildet** the picture	**bilder** pictures	**bildene/bilda** the pictures
et hus a house	**huset** the house	**hus** houses	**husene/husa** the houses

et land a land, country	**landet** the land	**land** lands	**landene/landa** the lands
et problem a problem	**problemet** the problem	**problemer** problems	**problemene/** **problema** the problems
et samfunn a society	**samfunnet** the society	**samfunn** societies	**samfunnene/** **samfunna** the societies

Irregular Noun Plurals

As in English, a number of nouns have irregular plurals. These irregularities can be sorted into four categories:

1. Vowel change
   (for example, **en bok** "a book," **mange bøker** "many books")

2. Lack of predictable ending, based on the general pattern
   (**en feil** "a mistake," **mange feil** "many mistakes")

3. Dropping unstressed **-e**
   (**en onkel** "an uncle," **mange onkler** "many uncles")

4. Anomalous endings
   (**et øye** "an eye," **mange øyne** "many eyes")

The most important are listed below, by genders.

Irregular En Nouns

Many family terms (**far** "father," **bror** "brother," **onkel** "uncle") are irregular, as are body parts. A general pattern is that nouns that end in **-el, en, -er** will often drop the -e- when adding endings. Nouns that denote occupations (**en baker** "a baker") have special indefinite plural forms (**bakere** "bakers").

Singular		Plural	
Indefinite	**Definite**	**Indefinite**	**Definite**
en ankel an ankle	**ankelen**	**ankler**	**anklene**
en baker a baker	**bakeren**	**bakere**	**bakerne**
en bonde a farmer	**bonden**	**bønder**	**bøndene**
en bror a brother	**broren**	**brødre**	**brødrene**
en far a father	**faren**	**fedre**	**fedrene**
en feil a mistake	**feilen**	**feil**	**feilene**
en fot a foot	**foten**	**føtter**	**føttene**
en lærer a teacher	**læreren**	**lærere**	**lærerne**
en mann a man	**mannen**	**menn**	**mennene**
en onkel an uncle	**onkelen**	**onkler**	**onklene**
en sko a shoe	**skoen**	**sko**	**skoene**
en støvel a boot	**støvelen**	**støvler**	**støvlene**
en sykkel a bicycle	**sykkelen**	**sykler**	**syklene**
en takk a thanks	**takken**	**takk**	**takkene**
en ting a thing	**tingen**	**ting**	**tingene**
en vinter a winter	**vinteren**	**vintrer**	**vintrene**

Irregular Ei Nouns

Many **ei** nouns (and their corresponding **en** noun forms) have a vowel change in the plural forms.

Singular		Plural	
Indefinite	Definite	Indefinite	Definite
ei/en bok a book	**boka/boken**	**bøker**	**bøkene**
ei/en datter a daughter	**dattera/datteren**	**døtre**	**døtrene**
ei/en hånd a hand	**hånda/hånden**	**hender**	**hendene**
ei/en mil a mile	**mila/milen**	**mil**	**milene**
ei/en mor a mother	**mora/moren**	**mødre**	**mødrene**
ei/en mus a mouse	**musa/musen**	**mus**	**musene**
ei/en natt a night	**natta/natten**	**netter**	**nettene**
en/ei ski a ski	**skia/skien**	**ski/skier**	**skiene**
ei/en strand a beach	**stranda/stranden**	**strender**	**strendene**
ei/en søster a sister	**søstera/søsteren**	**søstre**	**søstrene**
ei/en tann a tooth	**tanna/tannen**	**tenner**	**tennene**
ei/en tå a toe	**tåa/tåen**	**tær**	**tærne**

Irregular Et Nouns

Singular		Plural	
Indefinite	Definite	Indefinite	Definite
et barn a child	**barnet**	**barn**	**barna** (cannot use **-ene**)

et eksempel an example	eksemplet	eksempler	eksemplene
et kne a knee	kneet	knær	knærne
et museum a museum	museet	museer	museene/musea
et sentrum a center	sentret	sentrer	sentrene
et sted a place	stedet	steder	stedene
et teater a theater	teateret/teatret	teater/teatre	teatrene/teatra
et øye an eye	øyet	øyne	øynene

No Singular Forms

These two nouns below do not have singular forms in Norwegian. To refer to one sibling, one must specify either **brother** or **sister.**

Singular		Plural	
Indefinite	Definite	Indefinite	Definite
—	—	**foreldre** parents	**foreldrene**
—	—	**søsken** siblings	**søsknene**

16 Personal Pronouns

Personal pronouns refer to nouns or people who are not explicitly named in a sentence or phrase. As in English, pronouns have a subject form (e.g., *I*), an object form (*me*), and a possessive form (*mine/my*). In grammatical terminology, *first person* refers to the person or persons speaking; *second person* points to the person or persons being spoken to; and *third person* points to a party other than the speaker or the listener. Subject pronouns serve as subjects of sentences. They refer to the actors or doers of the verbs. Object pronouns are objects of verbs or objects of prepositions. The possessive pronouns refer to a person who "owns" an object.

Norwegian has more forms for the second person (*you*) than English, as it differentiates between singular and plural. Norwegian distinguishes between the subject and the object form of *you* and also uses **De,** a formal "you" pronoun. The use of **De** is currently dying out in most of Norway and is now encountered only in the most formal settings and in historical documents.

Subject Pronouns

	Singular	Plural
first person	**jeg** I	**vi** we
second person (informal)	**du** you	**dere** you all
second person (formal)	**De** you	**De** you

third person (masculine)	**han** he	
third person (feminine)	**hun** she	**de** they
third person (inanimate)	**den, det** it	

The formal pronoun **De** "you" is always capitalized. **Den** "it" is used for third person **en** and **ei** nouns; **det** refers to **et** gender nouns. The pronunciation of several pronouns requires special attention: **jeg** is pronounced /jæⁱ/; **De** and **de** are pronounced /di:/ and rhyme with **vi** "we"; **det** is pronounced /de:/—that is, the final *t* is silent. **Han** and **hun** have a short /ɑ/ and /ʉ/ respectively, although the spelling predicts long /ɑ:/ and /ʉ:/.

Example sentences that use subject pronouns follow (pronouns and their translations are italicized):

Jeg **kommer fra Polen.**	*I* come from Poland.
Kan *du* **forklare det for meg?**	Can *you* explain that to me?
Jeg kjøpte en bok. *Den* **var dyr.**	I bought a book. *It* was expensive.
Frank solgte huset. *Det* **var gammelt.**	Frank sold the house. *It* was old.
Hun **heter Aud.**	Her name is (*she* is called) Aud.
Vi **liker å lese norsk.**	*We* like to study Norwegian.
Vil *dere* **gå på kino i kveld?**	Do *you* (plural) want to go to the movies this evening?
Røker *De,* **Knudsen?**	Do *you* (formal) smoke, Knudsen?
Camilla og Cecilie var syke. *De* **kunne ikke være med.**	Camilla and Cecilie were sick. *They* could not come along.

Uses of Det

Det has many uses, and is not only used to refer to **et** nouns. **Det** may be used as a grammatical, place-holding subject in impersonal sentences where there is no specific reference to a person or thing:

Det snør.	It is snowing.

Det er mørkt ute.	It is dark outside.
Hvordan står det til?	How are you? (*lit.* "how stands it to?")

Det may introduce or point out the existence of something and is used to introduce all genders, singular and plural.

Det er en god bok.	It/that is a good book.
Det ligger fem blyanter på bordet.	There are five pencils on the table.
Det er min beste venn.	This is my best friend.
Det var en gang en gammel bonde.	There was once an old farmer.

Det can also refer to a clause or a verb.

De kan ikke komme. Det har jeg hørt.	They cannot come. That is what I heard.
Kan du snakke norsk? **Ja, det kan jeg.**	Can you speak Norwegian? Yes, that I can.

Non-Reflexive Object Pronouns

	Singular	Plural
first person	**meg** me	**oss** us
second person (informal)	**deg** you	**dere** you all
second person (formal)	**Dem** you	**Dem** you
third person (masculine)	**ham** him	
third person (feminine)	**henne** her	**dem** them
third person (inanimate)	**den, det** it	

The pronunciations of **meg** and **deg** use the diphthong /æi/ in the same manner as the subject **jeg** "I."

Object pronouns are used:

- as the direct object of verbs

Gro ser meg.   Gro sees me.

- as the indirect object of verbs

Gro gav meg bildene.   Gro gave me the pictures.

- as the object of prepositions

Gro snakker med meg.   Gro is talking with me.

- predicatively in some expressions

Det er meg.   It is me.

Since English does not differentiate between subject and object forms of "you," students of Norwegian must be careful to use **du** and **deg** appropriately.

Subject: Du   **Object: Deg**

Du må skrive det på norsk.   **Jeg skrev et brev til deg i går.**
You must write this in Norwegian.   I wrote a letter to you yesterday.

Ser du den pene jenta?   **Ser den pene jenta deg?**
Do you see the pretty girl?   Does the pretty girl see you?

Du får komme nærmere.   **Jeg kan ikke høre deg.**
You can come closer.   I can't hear you.

Third Person Reflexive Object Pronouns

	Singular	**Plural**
third person (masculine)	**seg** himself	
third person (feminine)	**seg** herself	**seg** themselves
third person (inanimate)	**seg** itself	

When the object of a sentence or phrase refers back to a third person subject, Norwegian uses a special reflexive object form of the pronoun. In all cases, regardless of gender or number, the form of the reflexive object is **seg**. Thus, depending on the subject, **seg** means "himself, herself, itself," or "themselves." When the subject is first or second person (*I, we, you*), Norwegian uses the normal object form (**meg, oss, deg,** etc.).

Third person reflexive object examples:

Han så på seg i speilet.	He looked at himself in the mirror.
Pål så på seg i speilet.	Pål looked at himself in the mirror.
Hun så på seg i speilet.	She looked at herself in the mirror.
De så på seg i speilet.	They looked at themselves in the mirror.
Solveig og Ingrid så på seg i speilet.	Solveig and Ingrid looked at themselves in the mirror.

First and second person object examples:

Jeg så på meg i speilet.	I looked at myself in the mirror.
Du så på deg i speilet.	You looked at yourself in the mirror.
De så på Dem i speilet.	You (formal) looked at yourself in the mirror.
Vi så på oss i speilet.	We looked at ourselves in the mirror.
Dere så på dere i speilet.	You (plural, informal) looked at yourselves in the mirror.

Possessive Phrases

For most of the forms of the possessive pronouns described below, the pronoun must agree in gender and number with the noun that is "owned."

Norwegian allows two forms of possessive constructions with pronouns. The two types have different stylistic flavors.

1. The nouns can precede the pronoun. In this type of phrase, the noun is in the definite form: **bilen hans** "his car." This pattern is more oral, concrete, and earthy than (2).

2. The pronoun can precede the noun, and the noun appears in the indefinite form: **hans bil** "his car." Compared to (1), this pattern sounds more formal, textual, and abstract.

While there is a choice for speakers and writers in using (1) or (2), the two may not be combined, with the possessive preceding the definite form of a noun (i.e., ***hans bilen***).

In Norwegian, as opposed to English and other languages, the same form of the possessive pronoun is used both attributively and predicatively. Attributive construction places the modifier adjacent to the word it is modifying (**min radio**); predicative construction uses the main verb to join the modifier to the word it modifies (**radioen er min**). Compare the Norwegian and English:

Attributive

Det er min radio. It is *my* radio.

Huset mitt er stort. *My* house is big.

Bordet vårt var dyrt.
Our table was expensive.

Predicative

Radioen er min. The radio is *mine.*

Det store huset er mitt. The big house is *mine.*

Det dyre bordet er vårt.
The expensive table is *ours.*

Non-Reflexive Possessive Pronouns

	Singular	Plural
first person	**min, mi, mitt, mine** my, mine	**vår, vår, vårt, våre** our, ours
second person (informal)	**din, di, ditt, dine** your, yours	**deres** your, yours
second person (formal)	**Deres** your, yours	**Deres** your, yours

third person (masculine)   **hans** his

third person (feminine)   **hennes** her/hers   **}**   **deres** their, theirs

third person (inanimate)   **dens, dets** its

The possessives **min, din,** and **vår** agree with the noun owned, as shown for **min** below:

En noun	Ei noun	Et noun	Plural nouns
stolen min/ min stol my chair	**klokka mi/ mi klokke** my clock	**bordet mitt/ mitt bord** my table	**stolene, klokkene, bordene mine/ mine stoler, klokker, bord** my chairs, clocks, tables

The possessives that end in **-s, hans** "his," **hennes** "her(s)," **dets** "its," **dens** "its," **Deres** "your, yours" (formal), and **deres** "their(s)" are invariable: they do not change forms to match the gender or number of the noun. The possessive **hennes** exemplifies the pattern:

En noun	Ei noun	Et noun	Plural nouns
stolen hennes/ hennes stol her chair	**klokka hennes/ hennes klokke** her clock	**bordet hennes/ hennes bord** her table	**stolene, klokkene, bordene hennes/ hennes stoler, klokker, bord** her chairs, clocks, tables

Third Person Reflexive Possessive Pronouns

	Singular	Plural
third person	**sin, si, sitt, sine** his/her own	**sin, si, sitt, sine** their own

When a third person subject of a sentence or clause "owns" the object, Norwegian uses the reflexive, a special form of the possessive pronoun. The forms **sin, si, sitt, sine** are used for any third person subject. This reflexive possessive pronoun agrees with the noun's gender and number (as with **min, mi, mitt, mine**). Notice that the subject can be singular or plural, and can refer to male or female owners. The English sentence, *John kisses his girlfriend,* is ambiguous—it could be John's girlfriend or someone else's. In Norwegian, the use of the reflexive possessive clarifies ownership:

John kysser sin kjæreste.	John kisses his (own) girlfriend.
John kysser hans kjæreste.	John kisses his (someone else's) girlfriend.
Hanson spiser appelsinen sin, pæra si, eplet sitt, og bananene sine.	Hanson is eating his (own) orange, his (own) pear, his (own) apple, and his (own) bananas.
Gro snakker med moren sin, tanta si, barnet sitt, og kusinene sine.	Gro is talking to her (own) mother, her (own) aunt, her (own) child, and her (own) cousins.
Lærerne mine leser sin bok, sitt ukeblad, og sine aviser.	My teachers are reading their (own) book, their (own) magazine, and their (own) newspapers.

Since the subject needs to "own" the noun object, a non-reflexive possessive is required within the subject; a sentence may not have a form of **sin** in the subject.

Per og vennen hans er i London.	Per and his friend are in London.

This sentence cannot have the subject **Per og vennen sin.**

These special reflexive pronouns only refer to third person subjects. For first and second person subjects, the reflexive form is identical to the non-reflexive form.

Jeg snakker med moren min.	I am talking to my mother.
Vi snakker med mødrene våre.	We are talking to our mothers.
Du ringte til faren din.	You called your father.

17 Determiners

Several types of words modify or give further grammatical details about nouns. Some grammar books include articles (English *a, the*) in this class, but in this book such articles are included in the descriptions of nouns (chapter 15). Other determiners include demonstratives (English *this, those*) that single out and point to specific items. Indefinite pronouns (English *some, any, none, each,* or *all*) are a heterogeneous group that refer to sets or subsets of items, limiting or defining which items are included in the focus of the statement.

Demonstrative Pronouns

Demonstrative pronouns single out specific items. English demonstratives include **this, that, these,** and **those.** In Norwegian, as in English, demonstratives can point to nearby or more distant items, as well as to singular or plural items. In addition, Norwegian requires agreement of demonstrative pronouns with the gender of the noun.

Note in the examples below that the demonstrative pronoun is used with the noun in the definite: **bilen, bilene, døra, dørene, huset, husene.** This most common form, combining the demonstrative pronoun with the definite noun, **dette bildet** "this picture," is called "double definite." Norwegian does allow indefinite nouns to follow demonstrative pronouns under certain conditions—as in abstract references (**denne innflytelse** "this influence") and in more formal writing.

	Near		**Far**	
	Singular	Plural	Singular	Plural
en/ei **nouns**	**denne bilen** this car	**disse bilene** these cars	**den bilen** that car	**de bilene** those cars

	denne døra	disse dørene	den døra	de dørene
	this door	these doors	that door	those doors
et gender	**dette huset**	**disse husene**	**det huset**	**de husene**
	this house	these houses	that house	those houses

Demonstratives can also stand as stressed words, without the noun: **Jeg liker denne bilen** "I like this car." **Jeg liker denne** "I like this (one)." The understood noun determines the gender and number of the demonstrative.

When the demonstrative introduces people or things that come immediately after a form of **være** "be" (predicative use of the demonstrative), the demonstrative is a neuter singular form, regardless of the gender of the noun being presented:

Dette er min sønn.   This is my son.

Det er mitt barnebarn.   That is my grandchild.

Det er fine epler.   Those are fine apples.

Dette er mine studenter.   These are my students.

Indefinite Pronouns

A small group of pronouns do not refer to a specific person or object, but rather have a more general reference. These have several forms, agreeing with the nouns they refer to or, in some cases, the nouns they appear with (functioning as adjectives).

all is used with **en** nouns

All mat er dyr i Norge.   All food is expensive in
                                    Norway.

alt is used with **et** nouns

Anna er lei av alt mas.   Anna is tired of all the fussing.

Alt by itself means "everything."

Jeg kjøpte alt!   I bought everything!

Det er ikke gull alt som glimrer.   Everything that glitters is not
                                           gold.

alle is used with plural nouns

På alle måter prøvde vi å beskrive ham.	We tried to describe him in all ways.

Alle by itself means "everyone."

Nesten alle i Norge snakker norsk.	Almost everyone in Norway speaks Norwegian.

allting "everything" (equivalent to **alt**)

Når enden er god, er allting godt.	All's well that ends well.

annen, anna, annet, andre "other(s)"

Det må gjøres på en eller annen måte.	It has to be done in one way or another.
Det er en annen sak.	That's a whole other story.
Man kan sende e-post til andre fra hele verden.	You can send e-mail to others around the world.
Alt annet er tøv.	Everything else is nonsense.

en "one," **ens** "one's." **En** is more commonly used than **man,** and can be used as the subject, as the object, or in the possessive form **ens.**

En kan bruke datamaskin til å finne ut status for ens bankkonto.	One can use a computer to find out the status of one's bank account.
En vet aldri om framtiden.	One never knows about the future.
Ens ord kan bli misforstått.	One's words can be misunderstood.
Det som alltid forbauser en er fattigdommen her hjemme.	That which always surprises one is the poverty here at home.

hver (for **en/ei** nouns), **hvert** (for **et** nouns) "each"

Det går bedre og bedre for hver dag.	It gets better and better each day.
Hun uttalte hvert ord nøyaktig.	She pronounced each word precisely.
Hvert tredje år reiser de til Norge.	They travel to Norway every third year.
Vi satt på hver vår stol.	Each of us sat on his/her chair. (We each sat on our chair.)
Hver sin smak!	To each his own!

ingen "no one, nothing." **Ingen,** when it stands by itself, means "no one." With a noun, it is equivalent to **ikke noen** "none, not any."

Det er ingen hjemme.	There is nobody home.
Jeg har dessverre ingen penger.	I unfortunately have no money.

ingenting "nothing"

Jeg har ingenting å gjøre nå.	I've got nothing to do now.

intet "nothing" is an archaic form, but might be encountered in formal or older writings. Current Norwegian uses **ikke noe.**

man "one" (only as subject of sentence)

Man lærer sjelden av historien.	One seldom learns from history.
Man kan si at vi dør som vi lever.	One can say that we die the same way we live.
Man skulle aldri stole på andre.	One should never rely on others.

noe has three alternative meanings

1. By itself **noe** means "something":

Jeg må si noe.	I have to say something.

Noe måtte gjøres med dette.	Something had to be done with this.
Det var noe som vakte oppsikt.	It was something that created a stir.
Det gjør ikke noe.	It does not matter.

2. Referring to mass (uncountable) nouns of any gender, **noe** means "some":

Vil du ha noe melk?	Do you want some milk?
Vi må dessverre kjøpe noe.	Unfortunately, we must buy some.

3. In questions and negative sentences, referring to **et** nouns, **noe** means "any":

Jeg kan ikke finne CD-en noe sted i byen.	I can not find the CD anywhere in town.
Har du noe brød jeg kan låne?	Do you have any bread I can borrow?
Har du noe håp om å finne ham?	Do you have any hope of finding him?

noen

1. By itself **noen** means "someone" or "anyone":

Det banket noen på døra.	Someone knocked on the door.
Kjenner du noen her?	Do you know anyone here?
Jeg så noen som gikk med krykker.	I saw someone who was using (walking with) crutches.

2. Referring to plural nouns (of any gender), **noen** means "some" or "any":

Jeg har noen bilder fra Sveits.	I have some pictures from Switzerland.
Vi har bodd her i noen år.	We have lived here for several years.

Hun har ikke noen penger.	She has no money.

3. In questions and negative sentences, referring to **en** or **ei** nouns, **noen** means "any":

Har du noen gang sett henne?	Have you ever seen her?
Hun hadde ikke noen makt.	She did not have any power.
Jeg har aldri fått noen forklaring på hva det betyr.	I have never gotten an explanation about what that means.

18 Adjectives

Adjectives are words that describe or modify nouns or pronouns. They can be used as predicates (e.g., "The man is *tall*") or as attributes ("the *tall* man"). Norwegian adjectives must agree in form with the nouns or pronouns they modify. Endings are generally added to the adjectives' base forms when the adjectives modify **et** nouns or plural nouns. The base form is the form found in dictionaries and corresponds to the form that agrees with singular **en** gender nouns.

Adjectives with Indefinite Nouns

The general pattern for indefinite nouns is shown below for the adjective **fin** "fine." Adjectives appear in their base form, without endings, for indefinite singular **en** and **ei** nouns, add **-t** for **et** nouns, and **-e** for all plurals. Exceptions to this general rule are discussed below.

En singular (no ending)	Ei singular (no ending)	Et singular (-t ending)	Plural (-e ending)
en fin maskin	ei fin kvinne	et fint hus	mange fine biler
a fine machine	a fine woman	a fine house	many fine cars
Maskinen er fin.	Kvinna er fin.	Huset er fint.	Bilene er fine.
The machine is fine.	The woman is fine.	The house is fine.	The cars are fine.

Note that this "indefinite" form of adjectives is used both attributively (**et fint bilde**) and predicatively (**Bildet er fint**).

Most Norwegian adjectives add endings according to this pattern. A list of common adjectives and their forms follows. Since the **ei** gender forms are identical with **en** gender forms, this list joins **en/ei** gender, and shows **et** gender, and plural.

En/ei singular (no ending)	Et singular (-t ending)	Plural (-e ending)	English
dyp	dypt	dype	deep
dyr	dyrt	dyre	expensive
god	godt	gode	good
hvit	hvitt	hvite	white
rik	rikt	rike	rich
rød	rødt	røde	red
sein	seint	seine	late
stor	stort	store	large
varm	varmt	varme	warm
våt	vått	våte	wet

Irregular Adjectives

Exceptions to this pattern are, for the most part, simple to state and learn. The explanations and examples given below deal with the most common exceptions.

1   The Adjective Liten "Little"

This adjective differs so greatly from the normal pattern that it leads the list of exceptions. Notice that the **ei** form is different from the **en** form.

En singular, liten	Ei singular, lita	Et singular, lite	Plural, små
en liten gutt a little boy	ei lita jente a little girl	et lite barn a little child	mange små gutter, jenter, barn many small boys, girls, children

2 Adjectives Ending in -ig

Adjectives that end in **-ig** (or the common ending **-lig**) do not add **-t** when they modify singular, indefinite **et** (neuter) nouns.

En singular (no ending)	Ei singular (no ending)	Et singular (no ending)	Plural (-e ending)
en hyggelig kveld a pleasant evening	**ei hyggelig hytte** a pleasant cottage	**et hyggelig barn** a pleasant child	**mange** **hyggelige folk** many pleasant people

A few other **-ig** adjectives are listed here. Note that this list combines all three genders in the singular:

En/ei/et singular (no ending)	Plural (-e ending)	English
gjensidig	**gjensidige**	mutual
høflig	**høflige**	polite
ivrig	**ivrige**	enthusiastic
kjedelig	**kjedelige**	boring
ledig	**ledige**	vacant, unoccupied, free
livlig	**livlige**	lively
nyttig	**nyttige**	useful
tidlig	**tidlige**	early
tydelig	**tydelige**	evident
årlig	**årlige**	yearly

3 Adjectives Ending in -sk

Most of the Norwegian adjectives ending in **-sk** do not add **-t** when modifying singular **et** nouns. The following chart shows the forms for these **-sk** adjectives:

En singular (no ending)	Ei singular (no ending)	Et singular (no ending)	Plural (-e ending)
en norsk bok a Norwegian book	ei norsk jente a Norwegian girl	et norsk skip a Norwegian ship	mange norske bilder many Norwegian pictures
en historisk begivenhet an historic event	ei historisk kirke an historic church	et historisk museum an historic museum	mange historiske steder many historical places

En/ei singular (no ending)	Et singular (no ending)	Plural (-e ending)	English
amerikansk	amerikansk	amerikanske	American
automatisk	automatisk	automatiske	automatic
nordisk	nordisk	nordiske	Nordic
praktisk	praktisk	praktiske	practical
svensk	svensk	svenske	Swedish
teknologisk	teknologisk	teknologiske	technological

Exceptions from the above pattern include single-syllable adjectives that do *not* refer to nationality: these take the usual **-t** ending. There are only a few such **-sk** adjectives: **frisk** "healthy," **fersk** "fresh," **morsk** "gruff," and **falsk** "false." This chart shows all forms for these adjectives.

En singular (no ending)	Ei singular (no ending)	Et singular (-t ending)	Plural (-e ending)
en fersk sitron a fresh lemon	ei fersk plomme a fresh plum	et ferskt eple a fresh apple	mange ferske pærer many fresh pears

En/ei singular	Et singular	Plural	English
barsk	barskt	barske	grim

falsk	falskt	falske	false
morsk	morskt	morske	gruff

4   Adjectives with No Endings

Adjectives with base forms that end in an unstressed -e do not add any endings.

En singular (no ending)	Ei singular (no ending)	Et singular (no ending)	Plural (no ending)
en stille dag a quiet day	ei stille natt a quiet night	et stille år a quiet year	mange stille netter many quiet nights
en moderne by a modern city	ei moderne utstilling a modern exhibit	et moderne samfunn a modern society	mange moderne hus many modern houses

5   Adjectives Ending in Stressed Vowels

A number of fairly common one-syllable adjectives ending in stressed vowels add -tt (instead of a single -t) when they modify singular et nouns. Note also that several do not add the normal -e for the plural ending. Adjectives that end in stressed diphthongs (mostly -ei) follow the standard pattern of adding -t for et gender singular.

En/ei singular (no ending)	Et singular (-tt ending)	Plural (-e ending)
en ny virksomhet a new undertaking ei ny avis a new newspaper	et nytt universitet a new university	mange nye skoler many new schools

En/ei singular (no ending)	Et singular (-tt or -t ending)	Plural (-e or no ending)
blå blue	blått	blå

brei broad	**breit**	**breie**
flau insipid	**flaut**	**flaue**
fri free	**fritt**	**frie**
grei straightforward, clear	**greit**	**greie**
grå gray	**grått**	**grå**
rå raw	**rått**	**rå**

The adjective **bra** "good" is invariant; it does not take any endings:

en bra gutt a good boy	**et bra barn**	**mange bra menn**
ei bra jente a good girl	a good child	many good men

6   Spelling Conventions for Adjectives

Adjectives often simplify their spellings, as do other parts of speech. In order to avoid three consonants in a row, a double consonant is usually reduced to a single consonant when an ending is added.

En/ei singular (no ending)	Et singular (simplified, -t ending)	Plural (-e ending)
en grønn plante a green plant **ei grønn pære** a green pear	**et grønt tre** a green tree	**mange grønne epler** many green apples
allmenn universal	**allment**	**allmenne**
sunn healthy	**sunt**	**sunne**
vill wild	**vilt**	**ville**
trygg secure	**trygt**	**trygge**
visuell visual	**visuelt**	**visuelle**

In order to avoid three consonants in a row, adjectives with base forms that end in **-tt** or another consonant plus **-t** do not add the **-t** ending:

En/ei singular (no ending)	Et singular (no ending)	Plural (-e ending)
glatt slippery	**glatt**	**glatte**
flott superb	**flott**	**flotte**
briljant radiant	**briljant**	**briljante**
brunett brunette	**brunett**	**brunette**
lett easy	**lett**	**lette**

When the base form of an adjective ends in **-el, -er,** or **-en,** the **-e-** often disappears with the addition of other suffixes. In many cases, a double consonant is simplified before the endings.

En/ei singular (no ending)	Et singular (-t ending)	Plural (simplified, -e ending)
beskjeden modest	**beskjedent**	**beskjedne**
gammel old	**gammelt**	**gamle**
sulten hungry	**sultent**	**sultne**
vakker beautiful	**vakkert**	**vakre**
åpen open	**åpent**	**åpne**

Adjectives with Definite Nouns

The tables and discussions above describe the agreement between indefinite nouns and both attributive and predicate adjectives. A special, simpler kind of agreement is required for definite nouns with attributive modification. This pattern, similar to English "the big house," will be described below.

The form of the adjective is invariant, but the rest of the phrase needs special attention. In simplest terms, the adjective's form is almost always identical to the indefinite plural form, usually ending in **-e** (the few exceptions are listed below).

The adjective phrase needs to have a freestanding definite article. These definite articles agree with the gender and number of the noun:

* **den** is used with **en** and **ei** nouns in the singular;

* **det** is used with **et** nouns in the singular;

* **de** is the definite article for all plural nouns.

Recall that Norwegian nouns in the definite use suffixed definite articles (**huset** "the house"). Below are several examples of definite adjective phrases:

Definite article	Adjective in definite form	Noun (usually in definite)	English
den	store	bilen	the big car
den	store	klokka	the big clock
det	store	huset	the big house
de	store	bilene	the big cars
de	store	klokkene	the big clocks
de	store	husene	the big houses

The definite form for **liten** "little" is irregular. For singular **en, ei,** and **et** gender nouns in the definite, the form is **lille.** For all plurals, it is **små.**

den lille gutten	the little boy
den lille jenta	the little girl
det lille barnet	the little child
de små guttene, jentene, barna	the small boys, girls, children

This kind of construction, in which there are two markings of the definite (**de** and **barna** in the last example), is the previously discussed "double definite." The noun can appear using the indefinite. Double definite construction is used with concrete nouns: **den norske kirken** refers to a church building that is Norwegian, in contrast to **den norske kirke,** which refers to the institution of the Norwegian church.

Det hvite hus designates "The White House" (the institution), but **det hvite huset** means only "the white house" (the house that is white). Several other constructions use this definite adjective form.

* Possessives:

min røde bil	my red car
den røde bilen min	my red car

* Demonstratives

disse store bøkene	these large books

* Set expressions

hele dagen	the whole day
halve natten	half the night
kjære venn	dear friend
jeg, arme synder	a poor sinner like me
midt på svarte natten	in the dead of the night

Comparatives and Superlatives

Normal Patterns in Comparing Adjectives

Most adjectives form their comparative and superlative forms following a pattern very similar to English. The English and Norwegian systems are listed below:

English standard	Comparative -er	Superlative -est
tall	taller	tallest

Norwegian standard	Comparative -(e)re	Superlative -(e)st
høy tall	**høyere** taller	**høyest** tallest
varm warm	**varmere** warmer	**varmest** warmest

stille quiet   **stillere** more quiet   **stillest** most quiet

Other Patterns in Comparing Adjectives

Most exceptions to this general pattern relate to the spelling or pronunciation of the forms.

1. Unstressed **-e** with endings of **-er, -el, -en** is often dropped when adjective endings are added.

Normal	Comparative	Superlative
sulten hungry	**sultnere** hungrier	**sultnest** hungriest
travel busy	**travlere** more busy	**travlest** most busy
mager lean	**magrere** more lean	**magrest** most lean

2. Several adjectives double the final **-m** when adding comparative form endings. This does not occur in the superlative form.

morsom fun   **morsommere**   **morsomst** most fun
                          more fun

3. Adjectives that end in **-ig** or **-lig** in the standard form have irregular superlatives. Where the normal pattern for the superlative adds **-est,** these adjectives add only **-st:**

hyggelig pleasant   **hyggeligere**   **hyggeligst** most pleasant
                           more pleasant

viktig important   **viktigere**   **viktigst** most important
                           more important

Irregular Comparative and Superlative Forms

Some of the most commonly used adjectives have comparative and superlative forms that do not merely add endings. These are similar to English **good, better, best,** or **bad, worse, worst.** Below is a table with these irregular adjectives:

god good   **bedre** better   **best** best

dårlig bad   **verre** worse   **verst** worst

ung young	**yngre** younger	**yngst** youngest
tung heavy	**tyngre** heavier	**tyngst** heaviest
liten little	**mindre** smaller	**minst** smallest
gammel old	**eldre** older/elder	**eldst** oldest/eldest
lang lengthy/long	**lengre** longer	**lengst** longest
stor big	**større** bigger	**størst** biggest
få few	**færre** fewer	**færrest** fewest
nær close	**nærmere** nearer	**nærmest** nearest

Adjectives Compared with Mer and Mest

As in English, there are a number of adjectives that form their comparative and superlative forms with **mer** "more" and **mest** "most." These include some adjectives that end in **-et** or **-ed,** some with more than one syllable that end in **-sk,** adjectives ending in **-s,** some compound adjectives, and some "heavy" or long forms.

elsket loved	**mer elsket** more loved	**mest elsket** most loved
fremmed foreign	**mer fremmed** more foreign	**mest fremmed** most foreign
sympatisk nice	**mer sympatisk** nicer	**mest sympatisk** nicest
avsides remote	**mer avsides** more remote	**mest avsides** most remote
selvsikker self-assured	**mer selvsikker** more self-assured	**mest selvsikker** most self-assured
interessant interesting	**mer interessant** more interesting	**mest interessant** most interesting

General Comments on Comparing Adjectives in Norwegian

Since all comparative forms end in **-e** (except those formed with **mer**), they do not take endings when they modify singular **et** nouns or plural nouns.

en rikere mann   a richer man

et større hus   a bigger house

mange eldre kvinner many older women

The superlative form can appear both with and without the **-e** ending that most definite adjectives use.

Kenneth er best. Han er den beste gutten i klassen.	Kenneth is best. He is the best boy in the class.
Denne oppgaven var vanskeligst. Det er den vanskeligste jeg har gjort.	This exercise was most difficult. It is the most difficult I have done.

In Norwegian, as opposed to English, one uses the superlative in contrasting two items:

Hvem er yngst, Knut eller Jenny?	Who is younger (*lit.* = youngest), Knut or Jenny?
Når er det varmest, i januar eller juli?	When is it warmer, in January or July?

19 Adverbs

Adverbs comprise a diverse collection of words and phrases, with a variety of functions and meanings. Adverbs (underlined below) modify and give more detailed information about:

- verbs: **Han løper <u>fort</u>.** "He is running quickly."

- adjectives: **Prinsessen <u>veldig</u> pen.** "The Princess is very pretty."

- other adverbs: **Han løper <u>utrolig</u> fort.** "He is running unbelievably fast."

They can also shape the meaning of an entire sentence, giving details on:

- time: **Magnus har <u>aldri</u> vært i Harstad.** "Magnus has never been in Harstad."

- place: **Kom <u>hit</u>!** "Come here!"

- manner: **Jeg forstår <u>ikke</u> hva du sier.** "I do not understand what you are saying."

- degree of an action: **Jeg sov <u>litt.</u>** "I slept a little."

- mode of interpreting the whole sentence: **Jeg er <u>jo</u> trøtt.** "I am certainly tired."

Many adverbs and adverbial expressions are time expressions and are discussed in chapter 25. Also see the discussion of interrogatives in chapter 21, since several adverbs are question words.

Adverbs Related to Adjectives

Many adverbs in Norwegian are related to adjectives. For these adverbs, the same form as the **et** form of the adjective is used. For example, the adjective **pen** "beautiful" is **pent** when it modifies an **et** noun (**et pent hus** "a beautiful house"). This same form is the adverb "beautifully" in **Fuglen synger pent** "The bird sings beautifully."

Adjective Base Form	Adverb
sein late	**seint**
	Toget kommer seint i dag. The train is coming late today.
høy high, loud	**høyt** high, loudly
	Kan du lese høyt? Can you read aloud (loudly)?
god good	**godt** well
	Petter skriver godt. Petter writes well.
stille quiet	**stille** quietly
	Sitt stille! Sit still (quietly)!

Here are some common adverbs formed from adjectives: **bra** "well," **dårlig** "poorly," **fast** "firmly," **fritt** "freely," **langsomt** "slowly," **langt** "far," **samtidig** "simultaneously," **sikkert** "certainly," **sterkt** "strongly, sharply," **særlig** "especially."

Common Adverbs

The list below gives meanings and provides examples for many common Norwegian adverbs.

aldri   never

Hun har aldri vært borte.   She has never been away.

alltid   always

> **Vi ringer alltid på søndager.**   We always call on Sunday.

da   then, at that time

> **Da vil vi forstå hele historien.**   Then we will understand the whole story.

før   before (in time)

> **Hvor bodde du før?**   Where did you live before?

hvordan   how

> **Jeg forstår ikke hvordan du kan gjøre så mye.**   I don't understand how you can do so much.

ikke   not

> **Han kan ikke se kirken.**   He cannot see the church.

lenge   for a long time, long

> **Har du ventet lenge?**   Have you waited long?

nå   now

> **Hva er klokka nå?**   What time is it now?

nettopp   just, exactly

> **Har dere nettopp kommet?**   Have you just arrived?

ofte   often

> **Vi er ofte i Tyskland.**   We are often in Germany.

så   then, next

> **Først laget vi mat, så spiste vi.**   First we cooked (made food), then we ate.

sjelden   seldom

> **Man lærer sjelden av historien.**   One seldom learns from
> history.

svært   very

> **Det er svært viktig å komme i god tid.**   It's very important to come
> on time.

Suffix -vis

The suffix **-vis** "-wise" forms many adverbs: **delvis** "partially," **forholdsvis** "relatively," **forhåpentligvis** "hopefully," **gradvis** "gradually," **heldigvis** "luckily," **leilighetsvis** "occasionally," **nødvendigvis** "necessarily," **rimeligvis** "reasonably," **sannsynligvis** "probably," **tydeligvis** "evidently," **vanligvis** "usually," **i årevis** "for years."

Modal Adverbs

Four Norwegian adverbs give a special reading or understanding to the sentences they occur in. They are called "modal" adverbs, are always unstressed, and come after the main verb in the sentence. It is difficult to give exact English translations, but the English equivalents below offer some sense of their meanings,

jo   certainly

> **Han kommer jo snart.**   He'll certainly come soon.

> **Du kan jo forstå meg.**   You can certainly understand
> me.

vel   probably (has the sense of "I suppose")

> **Han kommer vel snart.**   He'll probably come soon.

> **Det fins vel ikke en ordentlig hest her?**   Isn't there an ordinary horse
> here, anyway?

da   surely (gives emphasis)

> **Kom da.**   Come on already.

Hvem er hun da?	Who is she anyway?

nok   probably, perhaps (also with the sense of "I suppose")

Han er nok ikke tilstede.	I'm afraid he is not here.
Det blir nok snø på tirsdag.	There'll be snow on Tuesday, I guess.

Adverbs of Place and Direction

Several adverbs come in pairs. One word is used to describe a static position or a location ("in a place"), while the other adverb describes motion to or from a location. For most of the adverbs below, the "to a place" form is shorter than the "in a place" form. The table summarizes the forms for these adverbs.

To a Place		In a Place	
fram	**Fortsett å kjøre rett fram.** Continue to drive straight forward.	**framme**	**Du er framme om en time.** You will be there in an hour.
hit	**Vil du komme hit et øyeblikk?** Will you come here a second?	**her**	**Vennene er her.** The friends are here.
hjem	**Jeg gikk hjem.** I walked home.	**hjemme**	**Vi sitter hjemme.** We are sitting at home.
inn	**Han skulle komme inn.** He should come in.	**inne**	**Det regner så vi blir inne.** It is raining, so we are staying in.
ned	**Kjør ned bakken!** Drive down the hill.	**nede**	**Nede i dalen er det kjølig.** Down in the valley it is cool.
opp	**Dere må opp.** You must go up.	**oppe**	**Vi er allerede oppe.** We are already up.

| ut | **Vi gikk ut.**
We went out. | ute | **Barna leker ute nå.**
The children are
playing outside
now. |

When two of these adverbs are combined, **hit, her, dit,** and **der** precede the adverb they appear with: **hit opp, her oppe** "up here," **dit ut, der ute** "out there."

After a helping verb (like **vil** "will," **må** "must," or **skal** "shall"), Norwegians often leave off the main motion verb (**komme** "come," **gå** "go," **kjøre** "drive") when one of these adverbs is present. For example:

Du må hit is equivalent to **Du må komme hit.**	You must come here.
Dere må hjem nå.	You must go home now.
Jeg vil ut.	I want to go out.
Skal han inn eller ut?	Is he going to come in or go out?

Comparative and Superlative Forms of Adverbs

Regular Adverbs

Adverbs that correspond to the neuter form of an adjective (e.g., **pent** "beautifully") are compared using the same forms that the adjectives use. The adjective **fin** (with the forms **fin, fint, fine**) has in all genders the comparative **finere** "finer" and the superlative **finest.** Thus the adverb **fint** "finely" has the comparative form **finere** "more finely," and the superlative **finest** "most finely."

Hun synger pent.	She sings beautifully.
Han synger penere.	He sings more beautifully.
Vi synger penest.	We sing most beautifully.

Irregular Adverbs

If the adjective on which the adverb is based has irregular comparative and superlative forms, these forms are then used by the adverb as well. For example, because the adjective **god** "good" has the irregular comparative form **bedre** "better" and irregular superlative form **best** "best," the adverb **godt** also uses **bedre** and **best.**

Han synger godt.	He sings well.
Han synger bedre enn læreren.	He sings better than the teacher.
Han synger best.	He sings best.
Nina bor langt borte.	Nina lives far away.
Ida bor lengre borte.	Ida lives farther away.
Laila bor lengst borte.	Laila lives farthest away.

Following is a list of adverbs with their irregular comparative and superlative forms:

bra well	**bedre**	**best**
dårlig, ille poorly	**verre**	**verst**
fram, frem forth	**fremre**	**fremst**
gjerne willingly	**heller**	**helst**
godt well	**bedre**	**best**
langt far	**lengre**	**lengst**
lenge long time	**lenger**	**lengst**
lite little	**mindre**	**minst**
mye much	**mer**	**mest**
nær near	**nærmere**	**nærmest**

20 Word Order

Word order in Norwegian follows the same pattern as English in most cases; however, students of Norwegian need to pay close attention to the differences. Definitions of the sentence parts will make explanations clearer.

The subject of the sentence is generally a noun (**katten**), a pronoun (**de**), or a nominal phrase (**Det at mannen er kjekk . . .** "That the man is handsome . . ."). The subject carries out the action of the verb.

The verb gives the action or state of being. Every statement or question has a finite verb, that is, the verb form that indicates tense. The finite verbs are shown in boxes below:

Katten [**sover**].   The cat is sleeping.

Katten [**sov**].   The cat slept/was sleeping.

Katten [**har**] **sovet i mange timer.**   The cat has slept for many hours.

Katten [**kan**] **sove.**   The cat can sleep.

[**Kunne**] **du sove?**   Could you sleep?

Det [**ble**] **sagt at...**   It was said that...

The sentence's main clause (or independent clause) is able to stand alone, while a subordinate clause (or dependent clause) needs to be connected to a main clause. Subordinating conjunctions (for example **fordi, da**) are the joining element.

Adverbs and adverbial phrases are used to indicate the time, place, or manner of the action; for example, **i Norge** "in Norway," **for to uker siden** "two weeks ago," **hjemme** "at home."

In each of the examples below, the subject is underlined, and the ⟨finite verb⟩ is boxed.

Normal Word Order

The normal word order in Norwegian statements is: Subject + ⟨finite verb⟩ + rest of sentence.

Solveig ⟨snakker⟩ norsk.　　　　Solveig ⟨speaks⟩ Norwegian.

Det ⟨var⟩ en gang en mann som hadde en kvern ved en foss.

Once upon a time, there ⟨was⟩ a man who had a mill near a waterfall.

Espen og kjæresten hans ⟨bor⟩ i Oslo.

Espen and his girlfriend ⟨live⟩ in Oslo.

Vi ⟨har⟩ vært i Trondheim mange ganger.

We ⟨have⟩ been in Trondheim many times.

Du ⟨må⟩ lese norsk nå.

You ⟨must⟩ study Norwegian now.

Det første opplaget ⟨ble⟩ utgitt i Russland i 1939.

The first edition ⟨was⟩ published in Russia in 1939.

Yes/No Questions

For questions that request confirmation or denial of information, Norwegian puts the ⟨finite verb⟩ before the subject. Note that English often uses a form of the verb "do" in similar questions. See chapter 21 for a complete discussion of this topic.

⟨Kjøpte⟩ hun et nytt hus?　　　　⟨Did⟩ she buy a new house?

⟨Kan⟩ vi skrive det på engelsk?　　⟨Can⟩ we write it in English?

⟨Har⟩ du tenkt deg en tur til Norge?

⟨Have⟩ you planned on taking a trip to Norway?

⟨Ble⟩ bilen solgt i går?　　　　⟨Was⟩ the car sold yesterday?

Questions with Interrogatives

When questions are meant to elicit new information, they use the question words—or interrogatives **hva, hvem, hvor, hvordan, hvorfor,** and **når.** The finite verb follows the interrogative, which can be the subject, the object, or an adverbial phrase.

<u>Hvem</u> kommer ?	<u>Who</u> is coming?
<u>Hvem</u> ser meg?	<u>Who</u> sees me? (note that **meg** is an object)
<u>Hvem</u> ser <u>jeg</u>?	Who(m) do <u>I</u> see? (note that **jeg** is the subject)
<u>Hvor gammel</u> er <u>hun</u>?	How old is <u>she</u>?
<u>Når</u> kom <u>du</u> til Danmark?	When did <u>you</u> come to Denmark?
<u>Hva</u> har <u>Kristian</u> på seg?	What is <u>Kristian</u> wearing?
<u>Hvordan</u> har <u>du</u> det?	How are <u>you</u>?/How do <u>you</u> have it?
<u>Hvorfor</u> sitter <u>du</u> så langt bak i kirken?	Why are <u>you</u> sitting so far back in the church?
<u>Hvilken dialekt eller sosiolekt</u> skal brukes?	<u>Which dialect or sociolect</u> will be used?
<u>Hvilke dager</u> har <u>vi</u> norsktime?	<u>Which days</u> do <u>we</u> have Norwegian class?

Notice that the finite verb comes in the second position, when the phrase with the interrogative (**hvilke dager, hvor gammel**) is counted as position one.

Inverted Word Order

In order to draw more attention to an element in a sentence other than the subject, that element can take the lead-off position. This highlighted element can be an object, a prepositional phrase, or an adverb of time or place. In Norwegian, a subordinate clause can also begin a sentence. In all of these instances, the Norwegian sentence is *inverted,* that is, the usual order of the <u>subject</u> and the finite verb is reversed. The non-inverted order is <u>subject</u> + finite verb ; the inverted order is finite verb + <u>subject</u>.

Bøkene sine lot **han hjemme.**	His books, <u>he</u> left at home.
I dette nummeret av bladet blir **norsk belyst fra mange sider.**	In this issue of <u>the journal</u>, <u>Norwegian</u> will be analyzed from many angles.
I morgen tidlig skal **vi til Italia.**	Early tomorrow <u>we</u> are going to Italy.
Da jeg våknet, skinte **månen inn på gulvet.**	When I awoke, the <u>moon</u> was shining in on the floor.

Complex Sentences

Complex sentences contain a main clause (which can stand alone) and a subordinate clause (which begins with a subordinating conjunction).

Subordinate clauses start with a subordinating conjunction and continue with the order conjunction + <u>subject</u> + finite verb (as in simple statements without inversion). The examples below give only the subordinate clause:

Når <u>du</u> er **kommet fram...**	When you have arrived...
Da <u>de</u> var **ferdige...**	When they were ready...
Selv om <u>mange gamle former</u> er **blitt gjeninnført i bokmålet...**	Even though many old forms have been supported in Bokmål...
Før <u>jeg</u> legger **meg...**	Before I go to bed...
Siden <u>han</u> nå er **drept...**	Because (since) he now has been killed...
Fordi <u>borgermesteren</u> kom **fra** <u>Nord-Norge...</u>	Because the mayor came from North Norway...
Mens <u>Ingunn</u> holdt **på med det...**	While Ingunn continued with that...
Da <u>han</u> ville **besøke oss...**	Because he wanted to visit us...

Subordinate clauses keep the same word order, whether they precede or follow the independent clause. In these examples where the subordinate clause follows the main clause, the word order is still conjunction + subject + finite verb :

Han spiste *fordi* **han** var *sulten.*   He ate *because he was hungry.*

Hun ønsker *at* **hun** vinner   She hopes (wishes) *that she will*
gullmedaljen.   *win the gold medal.*

Ikke Placement

This section deals with the placement of **ikke** "not," as well as several other adverbs describing condition or frequency: **aldri** "never," **alltid** "always," **bestandig** "constantly," **gjerne** "usually, with pleasure," **ofte** "often," and **sjelden** "seldom." The placement of these words relative to the finite verb is the most important consideration here.

In straightforward, simple declarative phrases, **ikke** follows immediately after the finite verb :

Trygve drikker **ikke kaffe.**   Trygve does not drink coffee.

Trine kan **ikke drikke kaffe.**   Trine can not drink coffee.

Rune drakk **ikke kaffe.**   Rune didn't drink coffee.

Sissel har **ikke drukket kaffe**   Sissel has not drunk coffee for
på ett år.   one year.

Finn liker **ikke å drikke kaffe**   Finn doesn't like to drink coffee
om kvelden.   during the evening.

This general pattern is modified slightly when a pronoun immediately follows the finite verb . In this case, **ikke** follows the pronoun. Compare the following sentences:

Øyvind ser **Sara.**   Øyvind sees Sara.

Øyvind ser **ikke Sara.**   Øyvind does not see Sara.

Øyvind ser **henne.**   Øyvind sees her.

Øyvind ser **henne ikke.**   Øyvind does not see her.

If two pronouns follow the ⌈ finite verb ⌉, **ikke** follows both:

Bodil ⌈ **gav** ⌉ **ikke boken til Bjarne.**   Bodil did not give the book to Bjarne.

Bodil ⌈ **gav** ⌉ **den ikke til Bjarne.**   Bodil did not give it to Bjarne.

Bodil ⌈ **gav** ⌉ **ham den ikke.**   Bodil did not give it to him.

These patterns hold only when pronouns follow immediately after the ⌈ finite verb ⌉. Note that in sentences that use modal helping verbs, **ikke** follows the modal (the finite verb), and the pronoun follows the infinitive form.

Tommy ⌈ **kan** ⌉ **forstå Jenny.**   Tommy can understand Jenny.

Tommy ⌈ **kan** ⌉ **ikke forstå Jenny.**   Tommy can not understand Jenny.

Tommy ⌈ **kan** ⌉ **ikke forstå henne.**   Tommy can not understand her.

In questions, **ikke** follows the same pattern in relation to the ⌈ finite verb ⌉:

⌈ **Kan** ⌉ **ikke Tommy forstå Jenny?**   Can't Tommy understand Jenny?

⌈ **Forstår** ⌉ **ikke Tommy Jenny?**   Doesn't Tommy understand Jenny?

⌈ **Forstår** ⌉ **han ikke Jenny?**   Doesn't he understand Jenny?

⌈ **Forstår** ⌉ **han henne ikke?**   Doesn't he understand her?

Ikke Placement with the Imperative

Ikke can either precede or follow the imperative form in Norwegian:

Ikke snakk så høyt!   Don't speak so loudly!

Snakk ikke så høyt!   Don't speak so loudly!

Ikke in Subordinate Clauses

In subordinate clauses, **ikke** (and **aldri, alltid, bestandig, gjerne, ofte,** and **sjelden**) immediately precede (rather than follow) the $\boxed{\text{finite verb}}$:

Jeg var så redd at <u>jeg</u> ikke $\boxed{\text{torde}}$ **sette en fot i kjøkkenet.**	I was so scared that I dared not set foot in the kitchen.
Han sa at <u>han</u> ikke $\boxed{\text{ville}}$ **gå på kino i kveld.**	He said that he did not want to go to the movie this evening.
Mannen spurte om <u>jeg</u> ikke $\boxed{\text{trengte}}$ **hjelp.**	The man asked if I needed (did not need) help.
Kjell forstod meg selv om <u>han</u> aldri $\boxed{\text{har}}$ **lest norsk.**	Kjell understood me even though he never has studied Norwegian.

21 Questions

Questions with Interrogatives

In formulating questions, the speaker may use interrogatives like the English *when* or *how* to elicit new information: "*What* is your name?" Norwegian interrogatives are listed below:

Interrogative	Verb	Rest of Sentence	English
Hva	er	dette?	What is this?
Hvor	kommer	Marit fra?	Where does Marit come from?

Hva   what

Hva vil du drikke?	What do you want to drink?
Hva heter du?	What is your name? (What are you called?)

Hvem   who, whom

Hvem var i Stockholm i forrige uke?	Who was in Stockholm last week?
Hvem så du?	Whom did you see?

Hvor   where

Hvor bor du nå?	Where do you live now?

Hvor + *adjective or adverb*   how

Hvor gammel er du?	How old are you?
Hvor langt er det til Bodø?	How far is it to Bodø?
Hvor mange er klokka?	What time is it? (*lit.* How many is the clock?)

Når   when

Når pleier nordmenn å spise middag?	When do Norwegians usually eat dinner?

Hvis*/hvem sin/hvem sitt/hvem sine   whose

Hvem sin datter er hun?	Whose daughter is she?
Hvem sitt hus har du kjøpt?	Whose house did you buy?

Hvilken (singular **en** and **ei** nouns)
Hvilket (singular **et** nouns)   } which
Hvilke (plural nouns)

Hvilken film liker du best?	Which film do you like best?
Hvilket land kommer han fra?	Which country does he come from?
Hvilke bøker anbefaler du?	Which books do you recommend?

Hvorfor   why

Hvorfor lærer dere norsk?	Why are you learning Norwegian?

Hvordan   how

Hvordan står det til med deg?	How are you? (*lit.* How does it stand to with you?)

---

* **Hvis** "whose" is archaic. Use **hvem sin, hvem sitt**, or **hvem sine** instead.

Hvordan liker du deg i New Jersey?   How do you like (yourself in) New Jersey?

Yes/No Questions

The yes/no question does not request new information, but rather confirmation or denial: "Is your name Lene?" "Yes." These questions in Norwegian are signaled either through a change in word order or through a rise in intonation towards the end of the question. (This rise is steeper than the normal declarative rise heard in East Norwegian statements. See chapter 3 for more on pronunciation.)

Compare the word order in a statement and in a yes/no question:

Statement	Yes/no Question
Hun kjøpte et nytt hus. She bought a new house.	**Kjøpte hun et nytt hus?** Did she buy a new house?
Hun vil kjøpe et nytt hus. She wants to buy a new house.	**Vil hun kjøpe et nytt hus?** Does she want to buy a new house?
Mannen har ødelagt planen. The man has ruined the plan.	**Har mannen ødelagt planen?** Has the man ruined the plan?
Marit så dem i går. Marit saw them yesterday.	**Så Marit dem i går?** Did Marit see them yesterday?

22 Prepositions

Prepositions are used to connect a noun or pronoun (the "object" of the preposition) to another word or phrase in a sentence. Common prepositions in English are: *at, before, around, off, in,* and *with.* As in English, pronouns in Norwegian that are the objects of prepositions must be in the object case: **Jeg vil bli med henne** "I want to be with her."

Prepositions frequently have spatial meanings as their primary sense. *On* suggests a position above and supported by another object. In addition to these spatial meanings, the meaning of a preposition may be extended to deal with time or manner of an action.

The most common Norwegian prepositions with samples of their uses follow. Note that it is often useless to give an English translation for a given preposition that will always make sense. The prepositions that are used in time expressions will be discussed in chapter 25, and are marked below with an asterisk.

av   of, from, by

Vi fant et gammelt bilde av min onkel.	We found an old picture of my uncle.
i løpet av femtitallet	in the course of the fifties
et skuespill av Henrik Ibsen	a play by Henrik Ibsen
fra 1995 av	from 1995 onward
Jeg ble sparket av min beste venn.	I was kicked by my best friend.

blant   among, belonging to

blant annet (bl.a)	among other things

blant de fineste folk	among the finest people

etter   after, according to

Etter 1814 var Norge knyttet med Sverige.	After 1814, Norway was associated with (attached to) Sweden.

for   for, in order to

For meg er det en fordel.	For me, it is an advantage.
Mannen kjøpte boka for å lese den.	The man bought the book in order to read it.

fra   from

Hamsun var fra Nord-Norge.	Hamsun was from North Norway.
Fra 1991 til 1995 bodde vi i Frankrike.	From 1991 to 1995 we lived in France.

før   before (in time)

Hun kom hit før krigen.	She came here before the war.

hos   at, with

Jeg bor hos Larsons nå.	I live at Larsons now.
Hos nordmenn er det vanlig å spise middag klokka fire.	It is customary among Norwegians to eat dinner at four o'clock.

i*   in

I Finland snakker folk både svensk og finsk.	In Finland, people speak both Swedish and Finnish.
Jeg er født i 1948.	I was born in 1948.
Vi satt og ventet i en halv time.	We sat and waited for a half hour.

med   with

Jeg var med mange gode venner i kveld.	I was with lots of good friends last evening.
Jeg har litt med det å gjøre.	I have something to do with that.
Vi reiser med buss til Ålesund.	We will take the bus to Ålesund.
Gudrun er gift med Gunnar.	Gudrun is married to Gunnar.
Hun begynte med å beskrive norsk uttalen.	She began by describing Norwegian pronunciation.
Hvordan står det til med deg?	How are you? (How stands it to with you?)
Frokost serveres med en gang.	Breakfast is served at once.

mellom   between

Det oppstod en stor konflikt mellom stammene.	A large conflict arose among the tribes.
Butikken er stengt mellom klokka 10 og 12.	The store is closed between 10 and 12 o'clock.
Mellom oss sagt, var det dårlig gjort.	Just between us, it was poorly done.
Hva er forholdet mellom våre to skriftformer?	What is the relationship between our two written norms?

mot   against, towards

Bilen kjørte mot oss.	The car was driving toward us.
Han stemte mot EU medlemskap.	He voted against membership in the European Union.
Det går mot sommer nå.	It's getting to be summer now.
Da det led mot kvelden, krøp Askeladden under sengen igjen.	When it got towards evening, Askeladden crept under the bed again.

Mot all forventning, kom ikke Statsministeren til Slottet.	Contrary to all expectation, the Prime Minister did not come to the Palace.

om*   about, around, concerning

Boka handler om Norges historie.	The book deals with Norway's history.
Hva synes du om dette?	What do you think about this?
Biblioteket ligger om hjørnet.	The library is around the corner.
Jeg bryr meg ikke om henne.	I'm not concerned about her.

over*   over

Boka kostet over kr 250.	The book cost over 250 kroner.
Klokka er fem over tre.	It is five past three.
Unni svømte over til øya.	Unni swam over to the island.
Bussen reiser fra Bergen over Otta.	The bus travels from Bergen via Otta.

på*   on, in

Avisen ligger på bordet.	The newspaper is lying on the table.
Hvordan sier du det på norsk?	How do you say that in Norwegian?
Olsen er på biblioteket nå.	Olsen is at the library now.
På fredag er vi hjemme.	On Friday we are home.
på Island	in Iceland
på Hamar	in Hamar

til   to, until

Familien Bakke skal flytte til Tyskland.	The Bakke family is going to move to Germany.
Sønnen til forfatteren er sytten år gammel.	The son of the author is 17 years old.
Er du sterk nok til å si nei til det?	Are you strong enough to say no to that?
Vi prøver på å gjøre denne by til et bedre sted å bo.	We are trying to make this city into a better place to live.

under   under, during

Under krigen hadde vi svært lite mat.	During the war, we had very little food.
Under reisen måtte vi kjøpe en ny koffert.	During the journey, we had to buy a new suitcase.
Hunden lå under senga hele dagen.	The dog lay under the bed all day.

ved*   at, with, by

Det kan løses ved hjelp av myndighetene.	It can be solved with the help of the authorities.
Jeg er student ved Universitetet i Bergen.	I am a student at the University of Bergen.
Kommer du til å spise ved fem tiden?	Are you going to eat at around five o'clock?

Particles

A particle is a small word that can have a big impact on the meaning of a verb. Many particles in Norwegian look like prepositions, but do not have an expressed object.

A sampling follows, with verbs listed in the infinitive:

bli igjen	remain
drikke ut	drink up
finne opp	invent
finne seg i	tolerate
finne ut	discover, figure out
gi etter	give in
gi opp	give up
gi ut	publish
gjøre opp	settle an account
kjenne igjen	recognize
komme med	join
komme seg fram	succeed
komme seg unna	get away
lese opp	recite
lese ut	finish reading
lukke opp	open
pakke opp	unpack
si opp	to quit (a job)
snakke ut	finish talking
spise opp	eat up
være med	accompany
være til	exist

23 Conjunctions and Subordinate Clauses

Types of Conjunctions and Clauses

Conjunctions join several sentence elements. In English, as in Norwegian, there are two types of conjunctions. Coordinating conjunctions join two equal parts of a sentence and include *and, or, for,* and *so.* Subordinating conjunctions join unequal clauses and include *because, until, whether, when, if, while,* and *although.* Complex sentences contain a subordinate and a main clause. The main thought, action, or focal point in the sentence is expressed in the main clause and modified by a subordinate clause introduced by a subordinating conjunction. In compound sentences, two independent and equal clauses are joined by a coordinating conjunction.

In the following compound sentences each clause is underlined, and the coordinating conjunction is shown in boldface:

John comes from New York, **but** Tom comes from North Dakota.

Oslo is the capital of Norway, **yet** fewer than half a million people live there.

In these *complex* sentences, the main clause is underlined, the subordinate clause is in parentheses, and the subordinating conjunction is shown in boldface:

(**When** Norway was under Danish rule), governmental business was conducted in Danish.

(**Because** Norway was then joined with Sweden in a joint kingdom), it didn't become an independent country until 1905.

Coordinating Conjunctions

The Norwegian coordinating conjunctions are **og** "and," **eller** "or," and **men** "but." They can join whole phrases or clauses or parallel elements within the phrases or clauses. The additional conjunction **for** "for" can only join clauses. **Samt** "in addition to" joins parallel elements within a clause.

og joins two nouns.

Vi spiste bacon og egg.	We ate bacon and eggs.

In **Vi spiste egg og drakk kaffe** "We ate eggs and drank coffee," **og** joins two phrases. In **Vi kan skrive og snakke norsk** "We can write and speak Norwegian," **og** joins two infinitives. In **Åse er Pers mor og Kåre er hans far** "Åse is Per's mother and Kåre is his father," **og** joins two independent clauses.

Following are some sentences with **men, samt,** and **for:**

Vi hadde tenkt å dra til fjells, men det snødde for mye.	We had intended to head for the mountains, but it snowed too much.
Vi er bestandig omringet av engelsk språk: fjernsyn, Internett, kino og popmusikk, samt faglitteratur.	We are constantly surrounded by the English language: television, the Internet, movies, pop music, as well as professional texts.
Hun kunne ikke komme for hun var syk.	She couldn't come for she was sick.

Several conjunctions are used in pairs or series:

både . . . og	**enten . . . eller**
både x, y, **og** z	**(h)verken . . . eller**
Både Ibsen og Kielland var norske forfattere.	Both Ibsen and Kielland were Norwegian authors.
Både Nordland, Troms og Finnmark er fylker i Nord-Norge.	Nordland, Troms, and Finnmark are all counties in North Norway.
Enten du eller jeg må ringe dem.	Either you or I must call them.

Vi drar til enten Finland eller Island til høsten.	We're going either to Finland or Iceland this fall.
Det er hverken fugl eller fisk.	It is neither fish nor fowl.
Jeg vet hverken ut eller inn.	I don't know whether I'm coming or going.

Subordinating Conjunctions

There are a large number of subordinating conjunctions in Norwegian, so it is helpful to divide them into groups according to function. Make sure to note changes in main clause word order when a subordinate clause begins the sentence.

General

at   that (may be omitted in many cases)

Han sier (at) han er syk.	He says (that) he is sick.
Hvorfor tror du at studentene kan tysk?	Why do you think the students speak German?
Jeg kjente (at) dette var det jeg ville ha ut av livet.	I felt (that) this was what I wanted to get out of life.

Conjunctions of cause/effect

da   as

fordi   because

Vi spiste fordi vi var sultne.	We ate because we were hungry.

siden   since

Siden vi var sultne, spiste vi.	Since we were hungry, we ate.

ettersom   since

Conjunctions of condition

dersom   in the case that

hvis   if

Hvis du ikke har noe å gjøre på lørdag, ring oss.	If you don't have anything to do on Saturday, call us.

med mindre   unless

om   if, whether

Jeg vet ikke om hun er norsk.	I don't know if she is Norwegian.
Per spurte om hun var norsk.	Per asked whether she was Norwegian.

Conjunctions of concession

skjønt   although

enskjønt   although

selv om   even if, even though

Ole holdt foredrag selv om han var forkjølet.	Ole gave his lecture, even though he had a cold.

Conjunctions of time

da   when

De flyttet til Tromsø da Mari var atten år.	They moved to Tromsø when Mari was eighteen.

når   when(ever)

Når vi er trøtte, sover vi.	When we are tired, we sleep.

etter at   after

Line forstod hva de mente etter at de forklarte det flere ganger.	Line understood what they had in mind after they explained it several times.

før   before

Før vi gikk ut, kledde vi på oss.	Before we went out, we got dressed.

innen   before, until

Innen jeg reiser, må jeg skrive stilen ferdig.	Before I leave, I have to finish writing my essay.

mens   while

Det er vanskelig å snakke i telefon mens du kjører bil.	It's hard to talk on the phone while you are driving (a car).

fra   from, forth

Fra han var ung, snakket han nederlandsk.	He has spoken Dutch since he was young.

så lenge som   as long as

Conjunctions of purpose

for at   so that

Jeg ser ingen fare for at Norge skal bli et fattig land.	I do not see any risk of Norway becoming a poor country.

så   so that

Forfatteren skrev døgnet rundt så at boka skulle bli ferdig før han drog til Hawaii.	The author was writing around the clock so that the book would be done before he left for Hawaii.

Conjunctions of consequence

så   so

Han var trøtt så han gikk hjem.	He was tired, so he went home.

så at   so that

Hun er på permisjon, så lite gjøres nåfortiden på kontoret.	She's on leave, so little is done now at the office.

slik at   such that

Det er ikke noen vits i å klippe filmen slik at den kan få en 15-års grense.	There is no point in cutting the film so it can get a rating for fifteen-year-olds.

Conjunctions of comparison

enn   than

Det var varmere i Norge enn jeg hadde trodd.	It was warmer in Norway than I had thought.

jo . . . desto   the . . . the

Jo mer du prater, desto mindre hører jeg på.	The more you prattle, the less I listen.

jo . . . jo   the . . . the

Jo flere jo bedre.	The more the merrier.

liksom/likesom   like

Marit har krøllete hår liksom du.	Marit has curly hair like you.

som   as, like

Du må gjøre som jeg sier.	You must do as I say.

som om   as if

> **Han later som om han er full.**   He's pretending he is drunk.

så ... som   as ... as

> **Jeg er ikke så flink som du.**   I'm not as smart as you.

24 Numbers

Cardinal Numbers

The system for counting and numbering in Norway allows for an older system side-by-side with a newer one. The older system often puts single units before tens, as in the English rhyme about "4 and 20 blackbirds." In addition to this variety of order, Norwegians use two forms for 7 (**sju/syv**), 20 (**tjue/tyve**), and 30 (**tretti/tredve**). Although the forms **syv, tyve,** and **tredve** are no longer officially accepted by the Norwegian Language Council, many older texts and speakers still use them. The chart below lists the newer system preceding the slash.

1	**én, ei, ett**	12	**tolv** /tåll/
2	**to**	13	**tretten**
3	**tre**	14	**fjorten**
4	**fire**	15	**femten**
5	**fem**	16	**seksten** /sæ^{i}sten/
6	**seks**	17	**sytten** /søtten/
7	**sju/syv**	18	**atten**
8	**åtte**	19	**nitten**
9	**ni**	20	**tjue** /çɵe/ /**tyve**
10	**ti**	21	**tjueen/enogtyve**
11	**elleve**	22	**tjueto/toogtyve**

23	tjuetre/treogtyve	80	åtti
30	tretti/tredve	90	nitti
35	trettifem/femogtredve	100	ett hundre
37	trettisju/syvogtredve	200	tohundre
40	førti	430	fire hundre og tretti
50	femti	1 000	ett tusem
60	seksti	1 000 000	en million
70	sytti /søtti/	1.000.000.000	en milliard

Large numbers in English are written out with commas separating groups of three digits. Norwegians use either a space or a dot for separation. In official orthography, when the unit is placed before tens, the word **og** "and" joins the two elements, without a space (e.g., **treogfemti** = 53). For ease of reading, many writers use spaces (**tre og femti**).

Ordinal Numbers

Ordinal numbers (like "first, fiftieth") are used to place items in a specific order. For most numbers over seventh, ordinals add **-ende** or **-de** (for the teens that already end in **-en**). The smaller numbers have somewhat irregular forms, although **-te** is the ending for many. When writing ordinals with digits, it is common to put a period after the last digit (e.g., 3. = third).

1. (first)	**første**	7.	**sjuende** /ʃʉːente/ **syvende**
2.	**annen, annet, andre**	8.	**åttende**
3.	**tredje**	9.	**niende**
4.	**fjerde** /fjære/	10.	**tiende**
5.	**femte**	11.	**ellevte** /ellefte/
6.	**sjette**	12.	**tolvte** /tålte/

13.	trettende /-ene/	40.	førtiende
14.	fjortende	50.	femtiende
15.	femtende	60.	sekstiende
16.	sekstende /sæ'stene/	70.	syttiende /søttiene/
17.	syttende /søttene/	80.	åttiende
18.	attende	90.	nittiende
19.	nittende	100.	hundrede
20.	tjuende /çuene/ /tyvende/	200.	tohundrede
21.	tjueførst(e)/enogtyvende	430.	fire hundre og
22.	tjueandre/toogtyvende		trettiende
23.	tjuetredje/treogtyvende	1 000.	tusende
30.	trettiende/tredevte	1 000 000.	en millionte
35.	trettifemte/femogtredevte	1.000.000.000.	en milliardte
37.	trettisjuende/syvogtredevte		

Fractions

Halv /hall/ "half" is an adjective, so it agrees with the noun it modifies: **en halv liter** "a half liter"; **et halvt eple** "half an apple."

Fractions with denominators between 3 and 12 have two forms, one with the ordinal and one with the cardinal number plus **del** "part."

⅓   **en tredel/en tredjedel**   ⅗   **tre femdeler/tre femtedeler**

⅔   **to tredeler/to tredjedeler**   ⅙   **en seksdel/en sjettedel**

¼   **en firedel/en fjerdedel**

Fractions with denominators greater than 12 use only the cardinal:

$\frac{1}{13}$ **en trettendel** $\frac{7}{20}$ **sju tjuedeler**

A special form can be used in Norwegian for 1½: **halvannen** (*lit.* = half of the second) corresponding to **en og en halv** "one and a half." For example, **halvannen time** "one and a half hours," **halvannet år** "one and a half years."

25 Time Expressions

Days of the Week

The names of the Norwegian days of the week are not capitalized. All are **en** nouns.

mandag	Monday
tirsdag	Tuesday
onsdag	Wednesday
torsdag	Thursday
fredag	Friday
lørdag	Saturday
søndag	Sunday

På mandag reiste vi.	On Monday, we traveled.
På tirsdag reiser vi.	On Tuesday, we'll travel.
Om onsdagene spiser vi ertesuppe.	On Wednesdays we eat pea soup.

Months

The names of the 12 months are not capitalized in Norwegian. Where the month name is stressed differently from English, an apostrophe precedes the stressed syllable.

januar	January
februar	February
mars /mɑːʃ/	March
april /aˈpriːl/	April
mai	May
juni	June
juli	July
august /aˈgust/	August
september	September
oktober	October
november	November
desember	December

Seasons

The nouns for seasons in Norwegian are not capitalized and are all **en** gender.

vår (våren)	spring
sommer (sommeren)	summer
høst (høsten)	fall
vinter (vinteren)	winter

Om våren er det pent i Norge.	Springtime (in spring) is beautiful in Norway.
I vinter var det temmelig kaldt her.	This (last) winter it was quite cold here.
Til høsten skal vi til Danmark.	This (coming) fall, we're going to Denmark.

Writing Dates in Norwegian

The conventions for writing dates in Norwegian are as follows (using March 8, 1998):

I dag er det den åttende mars.	Today it is the eighth of March.
den 8. mars 1998	March 8, 1998
8.3.1998	3/8/98

Divisions of Time

sekund (et)	second
minutt (et)	minute
time (en)	hour
en halv time	half an hour
kvarter (et)	quarter of an hour
morgen (en)	morning
middag (en)	noon
formiddag (en)	midmorning
ettermiddag (en)	afternoon
aften (en)	afternoon
kveld (en)	evening

natt (en/ei), netter	night, nights
dag (en)	a day
døgn (et)	24-hour period
uke (en/ei)	week
måned (en)	month
årstid (en/ei)	season
år (et), år	year, years
tiår (et)	decade
århundre (et)	century

Expressions of Time

nå	now
i dag	today
i morges	this morning
i ettermiddag	this afternoon
i kveld /kvell/	this evening
i går	yesterday
i morgen /mårn/	tomorrow
i morgen tidlig	early (in the day) tomorrow
i år	this year
i sommer	this (last) summer
i fjor	last year
om dagen	during the day
om kvelden	during the evening

om høsten	in fall
hele dagen	all day
hele året	all year
neste uke	next week
i forrige uke	last week
for en time siden	an hour ago
for to år siden	two years ago
tre dager seinere	three days later
10 minutter tidligere	10 minutes earlier
om en uke	in a week
om tre dager	in three days
ikke på fire dager	not for four days
ikke på en uke	not for a week
ved seks-tiden	around six o'clock

The most important (and often misused by speakers of English) prepositions used in time expressions are listed here:

Om points to an event that will happen at a specific time in the future.

Kan dere ringe tilbake om én time?	Can you call us back in one hour?

I describes the period of time that an event spans.

Vi satt og pratet i to timer.	We sat and chatted for two hours.

På is used when a time period has elapsed *without* an event.

Harald har ikke blitt sett på tre døgn.	Harald has not been seen for three days.

På is also used to show how long something took to be completed.

Hun kan lese hele boka på fire timer.   She can read the whole book in four hours.

For . . . siden is used to describe the time elapsed since an event.

Vi dro av sted for tre timer siden.   We left three hours ago.

Telling Time

På means "before" while **over** means "after." While in English the focus in counting half hours is on the current hour, in Norwegian speakers look ahead to the next hour (**halv fem** = 4:30). The 10 minutes on either side of a half hour (e.g., from 10:20 to 10:40) are designated as before and after the half-hour period.

In formal settings, speakers note the exact minutes:

Den er fem tjuefem.   It is 5:25.

Klokken er ni null sju.   The time is 9:07.

The 24-hour clock is used in official and precise time-telling.

Flyet går klokken 17.25.   The flight leaves at 5:25 P.M.

Norwegians do not differentiate between A.M. and P.M., but can add **om formiddagen** "in the morning" or **om kvelden** "in the evening" when it is necessary to clarify the time of day.

There are several equivalent ways to ask what time it is:

Hva er klokken/klokka?

Hvor mye er klokken?   ⎱ What time is it?

Hvor mange er klokken?

The following list provides the full range of possible responses.

Klokken er sju. Klokka er sju.   It is seven o'clock.
Den er sju.

Klokken er snart sju.	It will be seven o'clock soon.
Klokken er nesten sju.	It is almost seven o'clock.
Den er fem over sju.	It's five past seven.
Den er ti over sju.	It's ten past seven.
Den er kvart over sju.	It's quarter past seven.
Den er ti på halv åtte.	It's twenty past seven (10 minutes to half eight).
Den er fem på halv åtte.	It's seven twenty-five (five minutes to half eight).
Klokka er halv åtte.	The time is half past seven.
fem over halv åtte	seven thirty-five (five minutes past half eight)
ti over halv åtte	seven forty, twenty to eight (10 minutes past half eight)
kvart på åtte	quarter to eight
ti på åtte	ten to eight
fem på åtte	five to eight
Klokken er akkurat åtte nå.	It is exactly eight o'clock now.
Klokken er ett (not **én**).	It is one o'clock.

Appendices

Common Verbs

Infinitive	Present	Past Tense	Present Perfect	English
angre	angrer	angret/angra	har angret	regret
arbeide	arbeider	arbeidet/ arbeidde	har arbeidet/ har arbeidd	work
arrangere	arrangerer	arrangerte	har arrangert	arrange
arve	arver	arvet/arva	har arvet	inherit
be	ber	bad/ba	har bedt	ask, request
begrave	begraver	begravde/ begrov	har begravd	bury
begynne	begynner	begynte	har begynt	begin
behandle	behandler	behandlet/ behandla	har behandlet	handle, manage
beholde	beholder	beholdt	har beholdt	retain, keep
bestemme	bestemmer	bestemte	har bestemt	decide
bestille	bestiller	bestilte	har bestilt	order
besøke	besøker	besøkte	har besøkt	visit

---

* Marks irregular forms, for example present tense forms that do not add the regular **-r** ending to the infinitive.

betale	betaler	betalte	har betalt	pay
betrakte	betrakter	betraktet/ betrakta	har betraktet/ har betrakta	view, regard
bety	betyr	betydde	har betydd	mean, signify
bevare	bevarer	bevarte	har bevart	save, maintain
bidra	bidrar	bidrog	har bedratt/ har bedradd	contribute
binde	binder	bandt	har bundet	bind
bite	biter	bet/beit	har bitt	bite
blande	blander	blandet	har blandet	blend, mix
bli	blir	ble/blei	har blitt	remain, become
bo	bor	bodde	har bodd	dwell
bre	brer	bredde/bredte	har bredd/ har bredt	spread
brekke	brekker	brakk	har brukket	break
brenne	brenner	brann	har brant	(intransitive) burn up
brenne	brenner	brente	har brent	(transitive) to set fire to
bringe	bringer	brakte	har brakt	bring
bruke	bruker	brukte	har brukt	use
bryte	bryter	brøt/braut	har brutt	break
burde	* bør	burde	burdet	should
by	byr	baud/bød/ bydde	har budt/ har bydd	bid/ command
bygge	bygger	bygde	har bygd	build

bære	bærer	bar	har båret	bear, carry
bøye	bøyer	bøyde	har bøyd	bend, conjugate
danne	danner	dannet/danna	har dannet/ har danna	form, create
danse	danser	danset/dansa	har danset/ har dansa	dance
dekke	dekker	dekket/dekka	har dekket/ har dekka	cover, set
dele	deler	delte	har delt	divide, share
dra/drage	drar/drager	drog	har dradd/ har dratt	drag, travel
drepe	dreper	drepte	har drept	kill
drikke	drikker	drakk	har drukket	drink
drive	driver	drev/dreiv	har drevet	operate, run
dyrke	dyrker	dyrket/dyrka	har dyrket/ har dyrka	cultivate, raise
dø	dør	dødde/døde	har dødd	die
døpe	døper	døpte	har døpt	baptize
eie	eier	eide/åtte	har eid/har ått	own
ete	eter	åt	har ett	eat (slang)
falle	faller	falt	har falt	fall
fare	farer	for	har faret/ har fart	fare, travel
finne	finner	fant	har funnet	find
finnes	finnes/fins	fantes	har fantes	be found, exist

fly/flyge	flyr	fløy/flaug	har fløyet/ har flydd	fly
flyte	flyter	fløt/flaut	har flytt	flow
flytte	flytter	flyttet/flytta	har flyttet/ har flytta	move
forberede	forbereder	forberedte	har forberedt	prepare
forby/forbyde	forbyr/ forbyder	forbød/ forbaud	har forbudt/ har forbydd	forbid, prohibit
forene	forener	forente	har forent	unite
foretrekke	foretrekker	foretrakk	har foretrukket	prefer
forklare	forklarer	forklarte	har forklart	explain
forlate	forlater	forlot	har forlatt	forsake, leave
forlove (seg)	forlover (seg)	forlovet (seg)/ forlova (seg)	har forlovet (seg)/har forlova (seg)	become engaged
fornemme	fornemmer	fornam/ fornemmet	har fornummet/ har fornemmet	perceive, notice
forstå	forstår	forstod	har forstått	understand
forsvinne	forsvinner	forsvant	har forsvunnet	disappear
forsyne	forsyner	forsynte	har forsynt	supply, provide
fortelle	forteller	fortalte	har fortalt	tell, explain
fryse	fryser	frøs/fraus	har frosset	freeze, feel cold
følge/følgje	følger/følgjer	fulgte/følgte	har fulgt/ har følgt	follow

få	får	fikk	har fått	get, receive
gi	gir	gav	har gitt	give
gidde	gidder	gadd	har giddet	manage to do something
gjelde	gjelder	gjaldt/galdt	har gjeldt	be in force, apply
gjøre	* gjør	gjorde	har gjort	do
glede	gleder	gledet	har gledet	please, make happy
glemme	glemmer	glemte	har glemt	forget
gli	glir	glei/gled	har glidd	glide
glimre	glimrer	glimret	har glimret	glisten
gnage	gnager	gnog/gnagde	har gnagd	gnaw
gni	gnir	gnidde/gnei/gned	har gnidd	rub
grave	graver	gravde/grov	har gravd	dig
gre (seg)	grer (seg)	gredde (seg)	har gredd (seg)	comb one's hair
greie	greier	greide	har greid	manage, deal with
gripe	griper	grep/greip	har grepet	grasp, seize
gråte	gråter	gråt/gret	har grått	cry, weep
gå	går	gikk	har gått	go, walk
ha	har	hadde	har hatt	have
handle	handler	handlet/handla	har handlet/har handla	act, shop, deal with
hende	hender	hendte	har hendt	happen

henge	henger	hang	har hengt	hang, droop (intransitive)
henge	henger	hengte	har hengt	hang up (transitive)
hente	henter	hentet/henta	har hentet/ har henta	fetch, bring
hete	heter	het/hette	har hett	be named
heve	hever	hevde/hevet	har hevd/ har hevet	raise
hilse	hilser	hilste	har hilst	greet
hjelpe	hjelper	hjalp	har hjulpet	help
holde	holder	holdt	har holdt	keep, hold
hoppe	hopper	hoppet/hoppa	har hoppet/ har hoppa	hop
huske	husker	husket/huska	har husket/ har huska	remember
hvile/kvile	hviler/kviler	hvilte/kvilte	har hvilt/ har kvilt	rest
høre	hører	hørte	har hørt	hear
håndhilse	håndhilser	håndhilste	har håndhilst	shake hands
inkludere	inkluderer	inkluderte	har inkludert	include
innføre	innfører	innførte	har innført	introduce
interessere	interesserer	interesserte	har interessert	interest
invitere	inviterer	inviterte	har invitert	invite
jobbe	jobber	jobbet/jobba	har jobbet/ har jobba	work
kjempe	kjemper	kjempet/ kjempa	har kjempet/ har kjempa	fight

kjenne	kjenner	kjente	har kjent	know (person, place)
kjøpe	kjøper	kjøpte	har kjøpt	purchase
kjøre	kjører	kjørte	har kjørt	drive
klage	klager	klaget/klaga/ klagde	har klaget/ har klaga/ har klagd	complain
klare	klarer	klarte	har klart	manage
kle	kler	kledde	har kledd	dress, suit one
klippe	klipper	klippet/klippa	har klippet/ har klippa	cut
knekke	knekker	knakk/knekte/ knekket	har knekket/ har knekt	crack, snap
koke	koker	kokte	har kokt	boil
komme	kommer	kom	har kommet	come
kose	koser	koste/kosa	har kost/ har kosa	make cozy
koste	koster	kostet/kosta	har kostet/ har kosta	cost; sweep
kreve	krever	krevde	har krevd	demand
kritisere	kritiserer	kritiserte	har kritisert	criticize
krype	kryper	krøp/kraup	har krøpet	creep
kunne	* kan	kunne	har kunnet	be able to
kvede	kveder	kvad	har kvedet	chant, sing
la	lar	lot	har latt	allow, let
lage	lager	laget/laga/ lagde	har laget/ har laga/ har lagd	make, create

late	**later**	**lot**	**har latt**	let, allow
le	**ler**	**lo**	**har ledd**	laugh
lede	**leder**	**ledet**	**har ledet**	lead
lege	**leger**	**leget/legte**	**har leget/ har legt**	heal, cure
legge	**legge**	**la**	**har lagt**	lay, place
leie	**leier**	**leide**	**har leid**	rent
leke	**leker**	**lekte**	**har lekt**	play
lekke	**lekker**	**lekket/lekte/ lakk**	**har lekt/ har lekket**	leak
lese	**leser**	**leste**	**har lest**	read, study
leve	**lever**	**levde**	**har levd**	live, be alive
lide/li	**lider**	**led/lei**	**har lidd/ har lidt**	suffer, wear on (time)
ligge	**ligger**	**lå**	**har ligget**	lie
ligne/likne	**ligner/likner**	**lignet/ligna/ liknet/likna**	**har lignet/ har ligna/ har liknet/ har likna**	resemble, look like
like	**liker**	**likte**	**har likt**	like
love	**lover**	**lovet/lova/ lovte/lovde**	**har lovt/ har lovet/ har lova/ har lovd**	promise, praise
lukke	**lukker**	**lukket/lukka**	**har lukket/ har lukka**	shut
lukte	**lukter**	**luktet/lukta**	**har luktet/ har lukta**	smell
lure	**lurer**	**lurte**	**har lurt**	wonder, dupe

lytte	lytter	lyttet/lytta	har lyttet/ har lytta	listen
lyve/lyge/ ljuge	lyver/lyger/ ljuger	løy/laug	løyet	lie, fib
lære	lærer	lærte	har lært	learn, teach
løpe	løper	løp	har løpt/ har løpet	run
låne	låner	lånte	har lånt	lend, borrow
male	maler	malte	har malt	paint; purr
melde	melder	meldte	har meldt	announce, report
mene	mener	mente	har ment	think, be of the opinion
merke	merker	merket/merka	har merket/ har merka	mark
misbruke	misbruker	misbrukte	har misbrukt	misuse, abuse
mislike	misliker	mislikte	har mislikt	dislike
motta	mottar	mottok	har mottatt	receive
møte	møter	møtte	har møtt	meet
måtte	* må	måtte	har måttet	have to, be obliged to
nyte	nyter	nøt/naut	har nøtt	enjoy
pipe	piper	pep	har pepet	whistle, pipe
prøve	prøver	prøvde	har prøvd	try, attempt
reise	reiser	reiste	har reist	travel; raise
rekke	rekker	rakk	har rukket	reach; be enough

rekke	**rekker**	**rakte**	**har rakt**	stretch
ri/ride	**rir**	**rei/red**	**har ridd**	ride (horse)
rive	**river**	**rev/reiv**	**har revet**	tear apart
ryke	**ryker**	**røk/rauk**	**har røket**	send out smoke, steam
røyke/røke	**røyker/røker**	**røykte/røkte**	**har røykt/ har røkt**	smoke (a cigarette)
se	**ser**	**så**	**har sett**	see
selge	**selger**	**solgte**	**har solgt**	sell
sende	**sender**	**sendte**	**har sendt**	send
sette	**setter**	**satte**	**har satt**	set, place
si	* **sier**	**sa**	**har sagt**	say, tell
sige	**siger**	**seig**	**har seget**	sink
sitte	**sitter**	**satt**	**har sittet**	sit
skje	**skjer**	**skjedde**	**har skjedd**	happen
skjelve	**skjelver**	**skalv**	**har skjelvet**	shake, tremble
skjære	**skjærer**	**skar**	**har skåret**	cut
skli	**sklir**	**sklei/sklidde**	**har sklidd**	slide
skrike	**skriker**	**skrek/skreik**	**har skreket**	scream
skrive	**skriver**	**skrev/skreiv**	**har skrevet**	write
skulle	* **skal**	**skulle**	**har skullet**	should, shall
skvette	**skvetter**	**skvatt**	**har skvettet**	start suddenly, splash (transitive and intransitive)
skyte	**skyter**	**skjøt/skaut**	**har skutt**	shoot

skyve	skyver	skjøv/skauv	har skjøvet	shove
slippe/sleppe	slipper/slepper	slapp	har sloppet	let go
slite	sliter	slet/sleit	har slitt	toil, wear out
slå	slår	slo	har slått	hit, strike
slåss	* slåss	sloss	har slåss	fight
smøre	smører	smurte	har smurt	butter, smear
sove	sover	sov	har sovet	sleep
sprekke	sprekker	sprakk	har sprukket	burst, split
springe	springer	sprang	har sprunget	jump, run
spørre	* spør	spurte	har spurt	ask
stige	stiger	steg/steig	har steget	climb
stikke	stikker	stakk	har stukket	stick, stab
stjele	stjeler	stjal	har stålet	steal
stryke	stryker	strøk/strauk	har strøket	strike, iron, remove, fail
stå	står	stod	har stått	stand, stand up
svi	svir	sved/svidde/svei	har svidd	burn, suffer
svike	sviker	svek/sveik	har sveket	betray, disappoint
synes	* synes/syns	syntes	har synes/ har syns	seem, think, be visible
synge	synger	sang	har sunget	sing
synke	synker	sank	har sunket	sink
søke	søker	søkte	har søkt	seek

ta	tar	tok	har tatt	take
telle	teller	talte	har talt	count
tenke	tenker	tenkte	har tenkt	think, intend
tigge	tigger	tagg	har tigget	beg, implore
tore	* tør	torde	har tort	dare
treffe	treffer	traff	har truffet	meet, hit
trekke	trekker	trakk	har trukket	drag, pull
trives	* trives/trivs	trivdes	har trives/ har trivs	enjoy, thrive
tro	tror	trodde	har trodd	believe
tvile	tviler	tvilte	har tvilt	doubt
tvinge	tvinger	tvang	har tvunget	force
velge	velger	valgte	har valgt	choose, elect
vente	venter	ventet	har ventet	wait, expect
ville	* vil	ville	har villet	want to, will
vinne	vinner	vant	har vunnet	win, gain
vise	viser	viste	har vist	show
vite	* vet	visste	har visst	know (fact)
være	* er	var	har vært	be, exist
ønske	ønsker	ønsket/ønska	har ønsket/ har ønska	wish, desire
åpne	åpner	åpnet/åpna	har åpnet/ har åpna	open

Prefixes and Suffixes

Prefixes

Norwegian uses a small number of prefixes, as does English, to modify the main word. The chart summarizes each prefix, with examples. Several prefixes are more international, having joined Norwegian as elements of loan words. These prefixes (like **multi-** and **ultra-**) are also often seen in English.

an-	**ankomme** arrive
be-	**beskrive** describe, **bety** signify
for-	**forstår** understand
fore-	**foreta** undertake
gjen-	**gjenlyd** echo, **gjensidig** reciprocal, **gjeninnføre** reintroduce
mis-	**mislike** dislike, **misbruk** abuse, **misforstå** misunderstand
om-	**omfavne** embrace, **omfattende** comprehensive, **omgi** surround
u-	**ugress** weed, **ugift** single, unmarried, **ujevn** uneven
unn-	**unngå** avoid, **unntak** exception
van-	**vanvittig** mad, **vantro** skeptical

Suffixes

The following chart shows suffixes, alphabetized according to the last letter of the suffix. If a student is reading and recognizes part of a word, finding the suffix listed here may help figure out the meaning. Both word-forming suffixes (like the English *-dom* "free + dom") and grammatical suffixes (like *-ed* "play + ed") are listed here.

-a	definite noun ending, **ei** gender singular	**jenta** the girl
-a	definite noun ending, **et** gender plural	**barna** the children
-a	variant past tense and participle ending for verbs like **å kaste,** which usually have **-et** endings	**å kaste, kaster, kastet** or **kasta, har kastet** or **kasta**
-d	past participle ending	**å prøve, prøver, prøvde, har prøvd**
-nad (en)	forms nouns	**en merknad** comment, observation
-dd	past participle	**å bo, bor, bodde, har bodd**
-e	indefinite noun plural for nouns	**en lærer, læreren, lærere, lærerne**
-e	infinitive ending for most verbs that are more than one syllable	**å finne**
-e	adjective ending for regular adjective modification of plurals	**hvite biler** white cars
-e	adjective ending for regular adjectives in definite constructions	**den store mannen** the big man
-e	adverb of location (as opposed to direction)	**hjemme** at home *cf.* **hjem** to home
-de	past tense of verbs	**å prøve, prøver, prøvde, har prøvd**

-ede	plural and definite past participles	**lukkede** shut
-dde	past tense of verbs	**å bo, bor, bodde, bodd**
-ende	present participle	**en gående mann** a walking man
-ende	ordinal numbers	**tiende** tenth, **femtiende** fiftieth
-ske	denotes female professions	**sykepleierske** female nurse
-sle	nouns from verbs, adjectives, nouns	**kjensle** sensation, from **kjenne** to feel
-ne	verbs showing a change of condition	**å hvitne** to whiten
-isme (en)	noun for distinct action or process "-ism"	**anakronisme** anachronism
-(e)ne	definite plural for nouns	**bilene** the cars **bildene** the pictures
-ete	past participle	**piggete** barbed
-inne (en)	denotes female professions, positions	**lærerinne** female teacher
-ere	comparative form of adjectives	**snillere** kinder
-ere	indefinite plural of nouns ending in **-er**	**lærere** teachers
-ere	productive verb forming	**engasjere** engage, get involved
-ere	comparative form of adverbs	**fortere** faster
-erne	definite plural ending of nouns ending in **-er**	**lærerne** teachers
-else (en)	noun forming from verb	**en begynnelse** beginning

-te	past tense	**å spise, spiser, spiste, har spist** to eat, eats, ate, have eaten
-este	definite form of superlative adjective	**den fineste jeg vet** the finest I know
-ig	adjective forming	**stilig** stylish
-(e)lig	adjective forming	**daglig** daily, **vitenskapelig** scientific
-messig	adjective forming	**regelmessig** regular
-aktig	adjective forming, having the quality of	**guttaktig/ gutteaktig** boyish
-ing	person from an area	**østfolding** someone from Østfold
-ing	noun forming from verb	**parkering** parking
-ling	diminutive or group noun	**elskling** darling, **tvilling** twin
-ning	noun forming from verb	**lesning** reading, study
-eri	noun forming, profession, workplace, collective activity	**fiskeri** fishing, fishery
-(i)sk	adjective forming	**luthersk** Lutheran, **nordisk** nordic
-sel	noun forming	**trivsel** enjoyment
-dom	noun forming	**fattigdom** poverty

-som	adjective forming	**hjelpsom** helpful
-en	definite singular of **en** noun	**dagen** the day
-skap	noun forming	**vennskap** friendship
-(e)r	indefinite noun plural	**biler** cars
-(e)r	present tense of verbs	**å bo, bor, bodde, har bodd** to live, lives, lived, have lived **å finne, finner, fant, har funnet** to find, finds, found, have found
-bar	adjective forming	**brukbar** usable
-er	noun forming name of profession	**baker** baker **lærer** teacher
-ær	noun forming	**millionær** millionaire
-s	possessive for nouns	**en bils** a car's **bilens** the car's
-(e)s	passive of verb	**det sies** it is said
-vis	adverb of manner	**heldigvis** luckily
-løs	adjective forming	**arbeidsløs** unemployed
-t	past participle of verb	**å spise, spiser, spiste, har spist** to eat, eats, ate, have eaten
-t	adjective form for **et** noun, indefinite singular	**et fint hus** a fine house
-(e)t	noun, definite singular, **et** noun	**huset** the house

-et	verb, past tense	**å snakke, snakker, snakket, snakket** to speak, speaks, spoke, have spoken
-et	verb, past participle	**å snakke, snakker, snakket, snakket** to speak, speaks, spoke, have spoken
-het	noun forming	**frihet** freedom
-est	superlative adjective, indefinite	**finest** finest
-est	superlative adverb	**fortest** fastest
-tt	adjective; **et** noun singular	**et nytt ord** a new word
-tøy	noun forming	**undertøy** underwear

Common Pitfalls
for English Speakers

The common mistakes described below are for the most part caused when English speakers follow English patterns and rules. By being careful to avoid these 12 common mistakes, students can make great strides towards more correct Norwegian. Note that sentences that are within asterisks are *wrong* and should not be used as models, but rather as examples of common mistakes.

1   Word Order

The most common mistake in both spoken and written Norwegian is neglecting to invert subject and finite verb when an element other than the subject starts a sentence.

> *I dag jeg er i Oslo.* ⇒ **I dag er jeg**   Today I am in Oslo.
> **i Oslo.**

The subject **jeg** is not the first element in the sentence, so the finite verb **er** must come before the subject. That process is usually called "inversion." (Conjunctions, however, can start the sentence without causing inversion.)

> **Men han er norsk.**   But he is Norwegian.

2   Infinitive of Verb Follows Modal Helping Verbs

After modal helping verbs like **skulle** "should," **skal** "shall," **ville** "would," **vil** "will," **måtte** "had to," **må** "must," **kunne** "could," and **kan** "can" (see chapter 7), the main verb must be in the infinitive form without the infinitive marker **å**.

Jeg må skriver et brev. ⇒ Jeg må skrive et brev.	I must write a letter.
Vi ville snakker norsk. ⇒ Vi ville snakke norsk.	We wanted to speak Norwegian.

3 Expressing -ing Forms in Norwegian

Norwegian does not have progressive verb forms corresponding to English "She is reading." The present or past tense expresses ongoing activities.

Han er spiser. ⇒ Han spiser.	He is eating.
Hun var sover. ⇒ Hun sov.	She was sleeping.

Norwegian also does not use the present participle of a verb to express an ongoing activity.

Hun er skrivende. ⇒ Hun skriver.	She is writing.

The most common Norwegian ways to express English -ing forms are:

1. Simple present or past tense:

Leif spiller fela.	Leif is playing the fiddle.
Leif spilte fela.	Leif was playing the fiddle.

2. A verb indicating position (such as sitte, ligge, stå) used with a main verb indicating the activity. The two verbs must be in the same tense and are joined by og "and."

Wenche sitter og leser romanen.	Wenche is (sitting and) reading the novel.
Nils satt og leste romanen.	Nils was (sitting and) reading the novel.

The expression holde på med å means "continues" or "is about to."

Frode holder på med å spise lunsj.	Fode is (continuing) eating lunch.

4   Finite Verbs Need a Tense

Norwegian draws a distinction between infinitive form (**snakke**) and the present tense (**snakker**). Students who rely too heavily on the English forms will be confused because in English infinitive forms are identical with the first and second person forms: "speak" is the infinitive and is also used in "I speak, you speak, we speak." Compare the following:

Jeg snakke norsk. ⇒ **Jeg snakker norsk.**   I speak Norwegian.

Jeg liker å snakke norsk.   I like to speak English.

5   Du, Deg or Dere

The various forms of *you* in Norwegian are often confused by English speakers. Norwegian distinguishes between subject and object for second person singular and plural where English does not.

Singular subject vs. singular object form

subject: **Du kommer fra Fargo.**   You come from Fargo.

object: **Vi kjenner deg.**   We know you.

Plural forms

plural subject: **Dere kommer fra Fargo.**   You (all) come from Fargo.

plural object: **Vi forstår dere.**   We understand you (all).

6   Definite Nouns Have Definite Suffixes

Definite forms of nouns use suffixed definite articles; not preposed separate articles as in English *the*.

det hus ⇒ **huset**   the house

de barn ⇒ **barna**   the children

7   Som/At/Hvem/Det—That

Although each of these words may correspond to English *that,* they may not be used interchangeably where "that" would be used in English.

Som connects a noun or pronoun with a clause that gives further information:

Han er en mann som jeg kjenner.

not

Han er en mann at jeg kjenner

or

Han er en mann hvem jeg kjenner.

The subordinating conjunction **at** connects a verb with a following clause.

Han vet at det er mandag i dag.   He knows that it is Monday today.

Jeg tror at han heter Per.   I think that his name is Per.

not

Jeg tror som han heter Per.

Hvem is the interrogative "who, whom."

Jeg kjenner en mann som heter Arnulf.

not

Jeg kjenner en mann hvem heter Arnulf.

Hvem er du sammen med?   Who are you together with?

When **hvem** is the subject in a relative clause, it must be followed by **som:**

Jeg så ikke hvem som snakket.   I didn't see who was talking.

The pronoun and article **det** corresponds to English "the" or "that":

det store rommet	the big room, that big room
Hvem er det?	Who is that?

8   Hvor/Hvordan—How Many, How Far

When English uses the interrogative *how* with an adjective or adverb, the corresponding Norwegian interrogative is **hvor**. **Hvordan** also means *how*, but is generally not used in conjunction with the adjective or adverb.

not

Hvordan mange venner har du?

Hvor mange venner har du?	How many friends do you have?

not

Hvordan langt er det til Stavanger?

Hvor langt er det til Stanvanger?	How far is it to Stavanger?
Hvordan staver du Kristiansand?	How do you spell Kristiansand?

9   Da/Når/Så—When/Then

Da can be a conjunction (*when*) or an adverb (*then*). Its function and translation is most often apparent in the word order. Note the appropriate English translation in each example shown.

Da telefonen ringte . . .   When the telephone rang . . .
(subject + finite verb implies **da** is a conjunction)

Da ringte telefonen.   Then the telephone rang.
(finite verb + subject implies **da** is an adverb)

Når is the conjunction that corresponds to *when* when the activity is in the present or future or *whenever* when the activity is a repeated action in the past.

Så as an adverb means *then, subsequently*. As a conjunction it means *so that*.

10   Synes/Tro/Tenke—To Think

Norwegian uses several different verbs where English uses only one, *to think*. Again, care should be taken to use the context-appropriate word in Norwegian.

Å synes is used when the speaker has experienced something and has formed an opinion based on that experience. One can argue with that opinion, but not with it as a fact.

> **Jeg synes filmen var spennende.**   I think the film was exciting (I saw it, and I found it exciting).

Å tro expresses something factual (whether correct or not). One can argue with the facts presented.

> **Jeg tror at han er i Bergen.**   I think that he is in Bergen.

Å tenke focuses on the mental activity of thinking.

> **Vi har tenkt å ta en tur til Grønland.**   We have thought about (considered) taking a trip to Greenland.

11   Gang/Tid/Time—Time

These three words are often confused by English speakers, although their Norwegian uses are very distinct.

Time, while it looks like the English *time,* means *hour* or *class period.*

> **Vi har ventet i en time.**   We have waited for an hour.

Gang means *time* only in the sense of *occurrence, occasion.*

> **Jeg var i Norge en gang for mange år siden.**   I was in Norway once (one time) many years ago.

> **Det var en gang et troll.**   Once upon a time, there was a troll.

The Norwegian **tid** covers English *time* in a much more general sense, with English equivalents *epoch, time period, passage of time.*

Du bør snakke norsk hele tiden.	You ought to speak Norwegian the whole time.
Hun visste ikke hva tid det var på natten.	She didn't know what time of night it was.
Tiden leger alle sår.	Time heals all wounds.

12   Word Pairs with Long and Short Vowels

Speakers of English often fail to differentiate between long and short vowels when they speak Norwegian. This leads to more blank stares from Norwegian interlocutors than other pronunciation inexactness.

The vowel in **tak** "roof/ceiling" is long: /tɑːk/.

The vowel in **takk** "thanks" is short: /tɑkk/.

Compare **mine** "my/mine" /miːne/ with **minne** "remind" /minne/.

Norwegian Names*

The Hundred Most Popular Female Names

Agnes	Borghild	Grete	Ingeborg	Kristin
Anette	Brit	Grethe	Inger	Kristine
Anita	Britt	Gro	Ingrid	Laila
Ann	Camilla	Gudrun	Ingunn	Lene
Anna	Cecilie	Gunn	Irene	Lillian
Anne	Eli	Gunvor	Janne	Linda
Aslaug	Elin	Hanne	Jenny	Line
Astrid	Elisabeth	Hege	Jorunn	Linn
Aud	Ellen	Heidi	Karen	Lisbeth
Bente	Elsa	Helene	Kari	Lise
Berit	Else	Helga	Karin	Liv
Bjørg	Eva	Hilde	Kirsten	Magnhild
Bodil	Gerd	Ida	Kjersti	Margit

* Information provided by *Statistisk Sentralbyrå*, Oslo

Mari	Mette	Reidun	Sissel	Tove
Maria	Mona	Rita	Siv	Trine
Marianne	Monica	Ruth	Solveig	Turid
Marie	Nina	Signe	Stine	Unni
Marit	Olga	Sigrid	Synnøve	Vigdis
Mary	Ragnhild	Silje	Tone	Wenche
May	Randi	Siri	Torill	Aase/Åse

The Hundred Most Popular Male Names

Alf	Einar	Helge	Jørgen	Magnus
Anders	Eirik	Henrik	Jørn	Marius
Andreas	Eivind	Håkon	Karl	Martin
Arild	Erik	Håvard	Kenneth	Morten
Arne	Erling	Inge	Kim	Nils
Arvid	Espen	Ivar	Kjell	Odd
Asbjørn	Finn	Jan	Kjetil	Oddvar
Atle	Frank	Jarle	Knut	Ola
Bjarne	Fredrik	Jens	Kristian	Olav
Bjørn	Frode	Johan	Kristoffer	Ole
Christian	Geir	Johannes	Kåre	Ove
Dag	Gunnar	John	Lars	Paul
Daniel	Hans	Jon	Leif	Per
Egil	Harald	Jostein	Magne	Petter

Pål	Rolf	Steinar	Thomas	Tore
Ragnar	Ronny	Stian	Thor	Trond
Reidar	Roy	Stig	Tom	Trygve
Roar	Rune	Svein	Tommy	Vidar
Robert	Sigurd	Sverre	Tor	Øystein
Roger	Stein	Terje	Torbjørn	Øyvind

Index